Oregon Uncaged

A TALE OF TWO-SIPS ON THE PACIFIC CREST TRAIL: OREGON

Crystal Hidde

DEDICATION

To my mom, thank you for the unwavering support throughout my life, and for taking every step with me along the way. To my husband, who encourages my adventurous spirit, and for lifting me up so I can fly. To my son, thank you for being my reason to breathe and to keep pushing forward every day...
 Left, right, left, repeat.

THE JOURNEY

ACKNOWLEDGMENTS

I would like to take a moment to acknowledge the PCTA and all of its volunteers. Thank you for working diligently to make the PCT accessible, safe, and enjoyable. A special thank you to the kind people who open their hearts and businesses; whom are the trail angels and the hiker resupply points. This journey would not be possible for many without all of the hard work and services you provide.

Thank you to my dear friend Jessica for helping me edit this book. I value your friendship so much, and I cannot express how much I appreciate all of your hard work, silly commentary, and the time you spent on helping me! I am forever grateful, and I owe you some tots!

PROLOGUE: FAMILY MATTERS

Just a few weeks before I would leave, my mom stopped by the house and we made a Costco run. I grabbed a large container of strawberries to dehydrate, but nothing else for the hike because I had been stock piling non-perishable foods over the last year. My resupply boxes were over flowing with food already. I actually had a box of extra food, so that my husband would be able to throw in more food to my next resupply box should I call for more. Which seems silly, because it altered the level of deprivation that I wanted to experience. More deprivation, less food. Less stuff! That is what I really needed.

After returning to the house, I drug my mom into our den, which had been turned into the "command center". Resupply boxes lined the back of the room. The boxes were organized neatly by resupply point and day to be shipped. Zip lock bags, empty cardboard boxes, lingering peanut butter to-go cups, and divided PCT maps littered the rest of the room. I excitedly started showing her the contents of the boxes.

"And look mom! Did you know that spam comes in a single serving pouch?" I presented her with the Spam as if it was an award.

She pursed her lips and shook her head side to side, as if she was witnessing something horrific.

"You don't have to carry all of that with you do you?" She sighed.

"Well, yeah, I mean, each box has five to seven days' worth of food" I told her.

She looked confused.

I tried to explain it to her again.

"Mom, it gets mailed to me, but only every few days."

3

My mother turned towards the open boxes, and calmly asked, "What about your water?"

"Oh," I said, "I'll carry that too. But I am going to have to find it along the way. But...."

My mom stood up and headed for the den door.

"I don't want to hear any more of it!" She said with utter disbelief and helpless worry.

It was obvious she was worried beyond measure, and she did not want me going on this trip alone.

"What if something happens to you?" She demanded to know.

I didn't have an answer for her. What if something *did* happen to me? But the question didn't cause me pain like it did my mother. And the truth is, this was the one time in my life she wouldn't be able to bail me out of whatever bad situation I came across, which she was really good at by the way.

When I was four, I was playing in the woods behind our home, and the neighbors dogs had gotten out of their yard. They were big dogs, especially large to a four year old little girl. The dogs went after me, and I tried to climb a tree but to no avail. I stood with my belly pressed against the tree, screaming and crying, and I remember my mom scooping me up and hugging me trying to calm me down.

When I was five or so, we went to the fair. I got on a kiddie ride, and when it was done I returned to the gate that I had used to board the ride, and my mom was gone. I screamed and cried searching through the sea of legs. Gazing past bottoms of snow cones and corndog boats through my tears. I didn't know there was an exit gate. Soon, my mom came running to me.

When I was in the first grade, I sat outside my teachers office and listened to my mom rip my teacher a new one, because the teacher told me I wasn't normal because I wrote with my left hand. My mom used cuss words I had never before heard in public. She later told me that I could write however I wanted to write; I could write with my toes for all she cared, just as long as I was writing the way I felt was right for me.

She has indulged my every dream, every desire, and has always taken my side when I needed a team mate or a fan. She has always been there.

I spoke about my plan of hiking the Oregon section of the Pacific Crest Trail, often. In fact, my mother bought me a new pack for my 33rd birthday. However, after seeing the resupply boxes and realizing the magnitude of what I was planning, something switched for my mother. She had officially joined the masses of other mothers and fathers, family and friends, who cannot stand the thought of, or fathom the reason behind a long-distance solo hike.

Her ninth and last baby was going to walk four-hundred thirty miles across the state of Oregon, and she was going to do it alone. Well, mostly alone. Charlie, my husband, would be going for the first eight days. But, my mom couldn't be there. She couldn't be sure I was sheltered from the elements, rescue me from a fall, or save me from wild animals. She wouldn't even be able to hug me when I needed it. She wanted to be supportive of this dream too but I couldn't make her understand my intense longing to be on the trail.

A couple of weeks before the hike I sent my mother a text message:

Me: How much does dad weigh?
Mom: A few pounds, why?
Me: I want to take him with me!
Mom: I am OK with that but did you talk to your sisters or anyone?
Me: Yes, they like the idea
Mom: Alright, I will bring him next time I come to town.

When My mom handed me my dad's ashes. I almost dropped the box.
"He is more than a few pounds!" I exclaimed, shocked.
When I got dad home I put him on the scale, eight pounds!
"Jesus! I can't carry that with me!" I told Charlie.

We both stared at the plastic container, our wheels turning. My gaze fixed on the seal-a-meal. My thoughts drifting back to when my father died 12 years ago...

My father had been diagnosed with Parkinson's disease quite some time before his kidneys began to fail. His tremors and overall lack of motor control became debilitating. He had the idea that if he increased his dosage of medications that treated the traits of the Parkinson's, he could regain control of his life: driving, sitting still, walking, controlling which way his head turned, etc.

My father also liked beer. Between the self over dosing of medications, coupled with alcohol, eventually, his kidneys began to shut down. For a long time my mom would transport my father forty-five minutes away to the dialysis center, where he would sit 3-4 hours at a time, three times a week. The routine took its toll on him, and the Parkinson's made his life that much more miserable.

I was living in Sacramento at the time when my mother called me to tell me that my dad had decided that death would be easier.

"Your dad has decided to go off of dialysis." My mother explained to me.

"Well, he can't just decide to go off of dialysis mom!" I scoffed, "His kidneys are getting worse, if he goes off of it he is going to...."

I couldn't finish my sentence. I could only cry into the phone.

My mother sighed deeply and then continued explaining.

"He has decided to wait to stop treatment until after his Birthday, but that will be the last time he goes to dialysis." She said.

I quickly tried to calculate how much time we had left with him. The doctors said that once dialysis was stopped, my father would die within two to three weeks, and September 5th, his birthday, wasn't that far away.

"Well, then I am moving home to take care of him." I said through my tears. My mother was arranging for a hospice nurse to come to the house a couple times each week. But, I was a certified nursing assistant at the time, and had worked in long term care homes. I wanted to be there to not only help provide the care that he deserved, but to be there as emotional support for him and my mother. I was in need of the family support as well.

I opened the black plastic box that contained my father, and pulled out the heavy plastic bag of ash. It was sealed with a twisty tie, the kind you'd find on a loaf of bread.

"Hi Dad," I thought and I twisted off the tie to open the bag. I turned my eyes away when I noticed bone fragments, and flashed back again....

I awoke to the sound of labored breathing. My father hadn't been alert for a few days. I rushed into his room, and after wiping his brow and applying lip balm to his lips, I kissed his forehead. The toxins secreting in his sweat made my lips burn and tingle. In the morning, mom called family and invited long time family friends to come say their goodbyes. I was outside when my mom retrieved me.

"Crystal, I think it is getting close to being time."
I rushed inside and hurried down the hall into his room. His good friend John and wife Therese were there. "We love you Murphy," they told him. I got comfortable next to him, laid my head on his chest, and closed my eyes. I listened to his heart beating softly, as his chest rose and fell with shallow unsteady breaths. Suddenly I couldn't hear his heart beat any longer. His chest rose with a deep gasping breath and then fell gently. I held him tighter as if not to let him slip away.

Charlie got a seal-a-meal bag ready, and I scooped my dad's ashes from the plastic bag that had entombed him for the last twelve years. After carefully funneling the ashes into the smaller plastic bag, Charlie sealed it, air tight.

"My god, do you think I am going to hell for this?" I laughed nervously. "No way will I be able to carry all eight pounds of him. Besides, he'd take up too much space!" I shook my head.

We put a pound of my dad's ashes into my Crater Lake resupply box, which my father in-law would mail out for me soon. I had picked out a place to take my dad's ashes that would be about a day hike outside of Crater Lake. It was the Oregon/Washington high point, and there was a small hill nearby that I would leave the trail to climb up, "Tipsoo Peak".

"When you get home, we will get a nice urn to put the rest of his ashes in, OK baby?" Charlie rubbed my back with one hand to comfort me.

1. IN THE BEGINNING

Despite my excitement, it was hard getting up and moving. I was sick to my stomach thinking about leaving the house and the dogs, my son, my normal. I made my way to the coffee pot and Charlie was in the kitchen making oatmeal. My stomach turned. I didn't think I could eat anything without vomiting. I took my coffee into the bathroom and placed it on the counter next to my flat iron. "Won't be needing that today," I kept repeating in my head, as I glanced at all the beauty products, makeup, and jewelry that cluttered the bathroom counter.

A few days earlier, Charlie had taken me to the jewelry store to let me pick out a band that I could wear on the hike. I always leave my ring at home on day hikes because I'm afraid I'll lose it out in the woods. Or, if something were to happen to me, my ring would still be at home.

At the mall, I chose a silver band that looked a lot like Charlie's wedding band. "There, now you will still be with me when I'm alone". I took off my diamond ring and replaced it with the shiny new band.

In lieu of makeup, I washed my face and poured on the sun screen. Holding back tears "wouldn't want to smear my sunscreen", I smiled at myself in the mirror.

"Today is the day," I whispered, "You're really going to do it, but do you really think you're going to make it?"

I stood there staring at my reflection, listening to my weaker-self raging an inner battle with my stronger-self. I looked up and stared into my own eyes, "Yes, I think you can".

I finally fixed a small bowl of oatmeal, and set it to the side. It was time to load up the packs into the truck and get to the trailhead in Ashland. It was just after 6am. Much later than we had hoped to leave.

After putting on my boots (laced just right, thanks to Anne at REI) I ran back to get a glimpse of one quote from a military survival manual my brother Bill let me borrow.
Charlie joked "Doing some last minute cramming?"
I was able to force out my words and a genuine smile, "I Just want to take a picture of a couple specific pages."

We threw our packs on. They were heavy, or so I thought at the time. I gave my pups a few last nose snuggles, and we headed out the door with an even heavier heart, to load up. I managed to choke down my oatmeal on the ride over. With my brother Bill's last piece of advice ringing in my head... "Slow down, don't panic, and be safe"...

Day one

We hit the trailhead at 7AM and it was already starting to feel warm out. Of course I picked the hottest week of the year yet to begin our hike. I originally wanted to leave around the fifth of July, but my brother Bill talked me into the first. He said it would be a good idea to do something different, and spend the Fourth of July on the trail, and that starting on the first of the month would give me a mental advantage to the mind game I was about to compete in.

So there we were, making our way into the twists and turns of the PCT on July first, in the midst of a heat wave. Charlie was carrying five liters of water, and I had three.

The trail made a steady climb up towards Pilot Rock for about four miles. I had done this section numerous times, but it seemed a little harder this time. Probably because my pack was so much heavier this time. Even though I felt as though I was carrying more than I could handle, I was excited to see beyond Pilot Rock, and I knew once we passed it I would feel like a new adventure had really begun. I was also looking forward to all the FLAT Oregon land everyone raved about in PCT forums and blogs.

We made our way up and down, up, up, flat. Then up, and down. Oh god, then back up! It always seemed like there were more ups than flat or down, and with the increasing heat from the sun, I was really starting to become grateful for any and all moderate terrain. I had spent many days in the gym and on the trails during the previous months. I had titled my workout routine: "Mission: Do not fucking die on the side of a mountain". I now couldn't decide if my pack was too heavy or if I hadn't trained hard enough!

We passed Pilot Rock and took a quick break to read over the water report and figure out how much further until our first water source. Looking at the map, we figured it was still a few miles ahead of us. The water report listed a "piped spring" on the trail. What does a piped spring even look like? I wondered.

Tall grasses and stubby oak began to take over the sides of the trail. I used my trekking poles to push the grasses to the side in front of my path as to not rub up against them. The last thing I wanted was to become camp host to the waiting ticks.
Suddenly, Charlie stopped behind me.
"Come here!" He called out.
Charlie was holding his eyelid open between his thumb and pointer finger. I came in for a closer examination.
"Don't blink! Don't move your eye!" I shrieked at him.

While I had been whipping back tall grasses and pushing past them, a small fox tail had shot out and somehow got up under Charlie's wraparound sunglasses, right up under his eye lid and against his eye ball! Charlie fixed his gaze on something distant to his far left, and I stared at the tiny barbs waiting to implant in his right eyeball.

I managed to grab it without pushing it in any further, and with a tweezer like motion, I pulled it away. I can't even imagine what would have happened if he had blinked one more time, or rubbed his eye. I was glad he had the sense to stop and calmly hold his eye open.

As we continued up the trail, I called back to him, "You know I would have made you a dandy eye patch out of a panty-liner and duct tape to get you to the ER." I giggled.

After a while we found the piped spring. It was marked with a warning sign that clearly stated we must treat the water. We exploded our packs in the shade of a tree. There we met our first thru-hiker (a hiker who is hiking the entire PCT from Mexico to Canada) his trail name was "Papa-Ratzi". He took our picture while we rested in the shade. He told us that he takes pictures of all the hikers he meets. Which meant he considered us to be hikers! The title made me squeal with delight inside! He also commented that he only carried two liters of water. One liter for every five miles. I wondered, "What does he do on the waterless 20+ mile sections?" He stayed for a few minutes and was off like a bolt. We remained there to refill our eight liters, and rest in the shade for quite some time.

The next few miles were more ups, a little flat, and then up again. I hiked in front of Charlie. My attention was consumed by trying to wrap my head around what I was really doing, and how long the journey was really going to be. Charlie tapped my pack with his trekking pole, waking me from my deep thought.

"Hey!" He sounded somewhat exasperated.

"Look!" and with his other pole he pointed down a spur trail, now behind me.

"What?" I asked, confused, turning to look at whatever it was he was showing me; annoyed because I wanted to keep moving!

"Our next water is down there!" he said, this time with more irritation in his voice.

It suddenly occurred to me how easy it was to miss a vital water source that wasn't located directly on the trail. I also realized that if Charlie hadn't been with me, I would have walked right passed it! Who knows how long it would have taken me to realize it, or if I would have been able to back track and find it on my own. I hung my head as we took the spur-trail to the pond.

We had covered eleven miles, and ended our day at the pond. Cold water poured from a plastic pipe, into a grassy pool that was buzzing with insects and full of slimy tall grasses. Charlie scouted out two trees in a nearby open field, and he decided that is where we would make camp. He slung his hammock between the trees, and I unrolled my bivy beneath it. We didn't talk much, and after dinner I laid there, watching the sun set. Charlie seemed troubled. I wondered if his silence was a result of worry or irritation over the fact that it was the first day and I was already making avoidable mistakes.

Day two

In the morning we found that another couple had also made camp near the pond. We headed out for the day before they got out of their tent. Not stopping to introduce ourselves, since they were still in bed, we skirted past. Sore from day one, and eager to get moving, we smiled and waved as we passed, but I took note of their ultra-light tent.

"Did they even have backpacks?" Charlie joked as we got back on the trail.

Steadier climbing revealed itself, and once the trail leveled out a bit we found a spot to have a quick mid-morning snack. My pack was starting to really weigh on me. It seemed so much heavier than the day before! It wasn't long before the couple from the pond went trotting past us as I sat on a log.
"How are you?" I asked them with a forced smile, focused on the fact that I could hardly see their packs, they were so small!
"Oregon is great! It's so FLAT!" The female cheered, practically running past me.

I wanted to trip her...

We continued towards Hyatt lake. Every thirty feet uphill felt like one-hundred. When we reached the Hyatt Lake outlet and bridge, I dropped my gear and took off my boots. I plunged my bare feet into the ice cold water, and let out a deep sigh. Suddenly the familiar pitter patter of doggy toenails came across the wooden bridge above me. Before I knew it, three pitbulls rounded the corner and came down to the water to drink, each of them taking turns to smell me and lick my face. Their human companion, "Micha", caught up to them and introduced himself. I reached out to the dogs, calling them back to me, and happily accepted more of their slobbery kisses. I was missing my dogs.
After a short visit, I watched as Micha walked the dogs back over the bridge. He loaded them up into his SUV, which was parked across from the creek, and then he drove away. Part of me wished we would have asked him for a ride to Hyatt Lake. But, I didn't want to skip any of the trail!
Charlie worked steadily to filter water and refill our containers. I continued to soak my burning feet, and have a snack. We watched as a solo female hiker came to the water's edge for a quick refill. She didn't stay long, and she didn't say much. Charlie and I seemed to take longer breaks than anyone we had ran into yet.
Before starting the hike, I felt like such a pro! But, I was constantly reminded by the weight of my pack, the exhausting heat, and my already sore feet, that I had bitten off more than I had ever chewed on before.
Charlie seemed increasingly uneasy. I couldn't tell if it was the heat, the physical pain, the building anxiety over me eventually going on alone, or if a mixture of all of the above was troubling him.

We reached the paved road that would lead us to a cabin at Hyatt Lake that a good friend was letting us use for the night. My boots hit the pavement hard, and sent burning pains up into my hips. The sun beat down on our faces. I prayed for a car to pass, so I could beg for a ride. We had less than two miles until we reached the cabin, but I felt like I could not take another step.

Soon, the sound of a car engine buzzed ahead of us. A small SUV passed us. I turned around, involuntarily flailing my arms, hoping the driver would see me through the rearview mirror and take pity on us.

Break Lights! The driver turned around and pulled over in front of us, it was Micha! Charlie and I climbed in to the rig. Less than a few minutes later we pulled in to the driveway of the cabin.

The shoulder straps of my backpack had worn raw spots near my collar bones. I showered, and applied antibiotic ointment to the burning wounds. Charlie cooked dinner, and we cracked open a couple of beers. Reluctantly, he began to tell me about what had been on his mind. Trouble had been brewing at home, and he wasn't sure if he should tell me at all.

"I don't want to ruin this trip for you!" He said.

"OK," I said, "Then we need to get home and take care of it."

"It isn't that simple babe," Charlie pleaded, "It isn't just about taking care of stuff at home! Look at all of the troubles we are already having. Maybe we should just go home and come back next year when we are more prepared."

My eyes started to well up, and a thick lump formed in my throat. "Charlie, we can go home and regroup., and take care of what we need to" I said calmly, but then started to cry, "But I am not ready to quit yet!"

Day three and four

After two days of lugging ridiculous amounts of gear up to Hyatt Lake, we returned home to take care of matters. Luckily we were still close enough to be able to arrange a ride back home to Medford from Hyatt Lake.

The fourth of July was spent with good friends, setting off fireworks in a cul-de-sac and grilling burgers; not suffering relentlessly on the trail as we originally had planned.

We also took the opportunity to dump about ten pounds of useless crap out of each of our backpacks, and exchange out other gear. By the time my sister Denise dropped us back off at the trailhead on the fifth of July, we were in good spirits. The best part though was it seemed the demonic heatwave had lightened up a little as well.

Day five

We picked up our resupply boxes at Fish Lake resort, doused ourselves in deet, and started up the trail. I was pleasantly surprised by the terrain. Maybe Oregon really was flat after all! Or maybe our packs were just more reasonable to carry without the kitchen sink dragging from behind.

While the temperatures were more bearable, the mosquitoes were relentless. We stopped periodically to take a breather, but it wasn't longer than a minute before Charlie would advise that we kept moving. Swarms of mosquitoes appeared the moment we stood anywhere much longer than that. As we walked, I pulled my head band over my ears to drown out the high pitched buzzing of the little blood suckers. A slight breeze would eventually come through, and the trail of mosquitoes would temporarily disappear. But I would happily take bugs over anything we had lived through the previous four days of our trek; mainly ungodly hot weather and over weighted packs. Things were really starting to look up!

We were still carrying "a lot" of water, but were drinking less due to the cooler temperatures. Our planned water resupply for the day was at Christie's spring. It was an eleven mile walk from where we had started the day. No Problem! Oregon is so FLAT!

I kept looking at the sky, thankful for the amazing weather, blue sky and a slight breeze. I could hear the rumbling of thunder coming from the east. I could see dark clouds starting to form in the distance, but the wind seemed to be keeping them at bay far to the side.

At Christie's spring we unloaded our packs, broke out our water filters, and began to refill. The water was cold, and the mosquitoes were thick. Soon, a voice carried over the bushes as a man appeared making his way to the spring, cussing. He immediately apologized when he saw me.

"Sorry if you heard any of that. Just cursing at these mosquitoes", he explained.

"The name is Seven, short for Seven Summits, if you're interested!". He smiled and nodded.

His voice was gentle, and I doubted anything he said with it could ever sound rude or harsh.

"No trail names, yet" I replied, "This is my husband Charlie and I am Crystal." I smiled back at him to reassure him I was not offended.

Seven was a thru-hiker, with another tiny ultra-light pack. He was an older gentleman with white hair, a soft voice, and he had walked all the way to this point from Mexico. Of course he had! He had already submitted Everest and six other of the world's highest peaks before finding us at this point. We, on the other hand had never been back packing before in our lives!

Seven wanted to know where we had planned on camping because he had "already claimed the campsite above the spring." He said he needed to stop for the day because he was still "rehabbing an old sports injury." Charlie and I had planned to push on a little farther, but we were hoping to find camp soon. There was another campsite listed in the Halfmile notes, a few miles up the trail. The wind was picking up, and the dark clouds were now moving in from the east and the west. Rain was on its way, I was sure of it.

After a total of sixteen miles for the day, we found a nice flat area off the trail to set up camp. Just as we put our packs down against a large log, it began to sprinkle rain. No big deal, I thought, that is why I brought rain gear. I had almost left my rain gear at home with a plan of mailing it to myself when I got a little farther north. But, I knew if I didn't pack it I would surly need it before I had it!

I handed Charlie the tarp and he began to hang it with some para-cord. No sooner, the loudest crash of thunder I had ever heard smashed through the thick tree cover above us. It didn't just start raining, it began to pour down heavy freezing cold rain. I ran to the packs and started stuffing what electronics I could inside it, hoping to keep them dry.

"OUCH!" Charlie yelped.

Something then stung against my cheek, and again. Hail! Marble-sized hail dropped down on us and bounced around the soft ground. It felt like nails were falling from the sky. Rain poured down. Charlie rushed to get the tarp pulled tight to shelter us. I stood there watching wondering what else I could do to help. I was holding myself in a tight hug and shivering, drenched to the bone, when Charlie turned to me and ordered me to get under the tarp.

My rain gear was still in my pack, but getting to my pack meant more time exposed to the cold wind and rain. Water began to accumulate at our feet, and it wasn't long before we were standing in a shallow pine needle stew.

"We need to get to higher ground!" Charlie exclaimed.

"I'll be right back!" He darted out from under the tarp, and he disappeared.

"CHARLIE!" I screamed out from underneath the tarp, trying to stop him before he could leave me there.

My cotton T-shirt and shorts were soaked through, and I was shivering violently. The wind and rain whipped against the tarp, and the thunder smashed through the trees above me. I peered out through the A-framed shelter desperately scanning through the thrashing vegetation, hoping to see him. But he was nowhere in sight, and I knew he was in no better condition than me. I crouched down and clutched my bare knees into my chest. The soles of my boots were disappearing under the rising water. After a few moments I desperately tried again to call for him. I yelled out his name in all directions, fearful to leave the cover of the shelter.

I screamed out, "CHARLIEEEE!"

It was pointless. I could hardly hear my self over the crashing thunder, hail, rain, and wind. Lightning lit up all around us. "I should be helping him." I thought to myself. But I didn't know where he went, and I knew that both of us running around out there was a worse idea.

I hunkered down trying to hold my self closely, a feeble attempt to conserve what core temperature I had left. Water poured off my hairline down my face. Suddenly, I caught a glimpse of Charlie's legs! He was running past the shelter! I yelled out, and he ran back to me.

"Are you shivering?" he asked, concerned.

I nodded my head yes, staring at him through fear in my eyes. Immediately, he grabbed my pack and tore into it.

"We need to get you warm!" He demanded.

He helped me get my rain gear on, and together we got our packs into large plastic trash bags. The water under our feet was now ankle deep. Charlie pointed out the area he had found.

"We need to move up there!"

He untied the shelter and we made a mad dash across the trail, which was now a small flowing creek, and I ran up the hill, chasing after him.

We each made two trips back to the flooded area to retrieve our scattered gear. The hail had stopped but the cold rain still poured down. After securing the tarp over higher ground, we shed our wet clothing, and put on dry base layers under our rain gear. The storm began to let up a little and Charlie immediately began working on building a small fire pit. Still shivering, I felt so helpless, but I was so grateful. Grateful for my husband. I found what dry wood I could, but wished that I was able to do more.

That night I sobbed quietly in my bivy. I didn't want him to hear my fears and insecurities pouring out. But the humbling realization and self-doubt was upon me with full force. A time was coming when I would be alone. The storms would come without Charlie. I was unsure if I would be able to move as fast as he did. Make shelter as fast as he did. Build a fire in the rain like he did. Protect myself the way he protected me.

Day six

The morning after the thunder storm, we moved slowly. Most of our clothing was wet and still drying on a log, steaming in the morning sunlight. We tried to let things dry and air out a bit before stuffing everything in our packs. Even though the sun was shining, the air was cold and water saturated the forest around us.

It was close to seven in the morning and the thru-hikers were already starting to dart up the trail. Seven walked passed our camp, and I waved to him.

"How'd you sleep?" he stopped and asked politely.
"Alright, we got caught in that storm!" I answered.

Who was I trying to kid? I didn't sleep all that well. I woke up several times in the night. I had been too cold and weary to even blow up my air mattress the evening before. The ground was hard and cold underneath me. I also slept as close as I could to the fire attempting to get warm. Which caused me to be paranoid that an ember would fly out of the fiery pit and melt my nylon minimalist bivy to my face! I kept picturing the nylon mesh withering like shrink wrap around my body, and rescue crews carrying me off the trail. I envisioned a scene similar to Han Solo frozen in carbonite...except bright orange with the REI logo permanently affixed to my chest.

Three more thru-hikers passed by. A couple, Ladybug and 2-Dots, and then a younger man who wore a cowboy hat, and had a much larger pack than the others. Maybe even larger than ours! This detail made me happy; confident. Finally, someone that looked like they actually packed something for the trip other than almonds and a flask for water!

He stopped.

"Hello", he said in an unfamiliar accent, "Are you just section hikers or are you PCT hikers?"

His thick foreign accent only distracted me momentarily from the slight irritation I felt from his question. I knew what he meant, but was somehow wounded that I was JUST anything. I felt reduced.

Well... I thought to myself. We ARE hiking on the PCT. However, it was a normal question. I shouldn't be offended. Everyone on the trail was interested to learn if you were hiking the entire 2650 mile trail, or doing a section hike. A section hike is committing to anything but the entire trail in one season. Most section hikers complete smaller bits of the trail on weekends, or some do longer stints at a time. We were section hikers, but we were still "PCT hikers", right?

"Just doing the whole Oregon section." I finally answered him.

"Oh," he said, "You are section hikers then".

There wasn't much more conversation that ensued, and he was off.

We loaded up our wet belongings, and began the day. Still chilled, I opted to leave my base layers on, under my hiking clothes. We had also decided to make it a short hiking day. I wasn't going to be insistent that we cover as much ground as possible, or argue that we had to do a fifteen mile a day to stick to the plan and get us to Crater Lake on time.

I was looking forward to getting to a new camp site, hopefully a dry one, and taking a load off in the sun. Ten miles sounded pretty good to me! The up side to being a section hiker is no one expects you to push fifteen to twenty mile days. Although it is common for a thru-hiker to cover as many as twenty-five to thirty-five miles day after day, or even fifty!

By the end of a little over ten miles, we found a wonderful campsite on a bluff that overlooked rolling hills, cliffs, and even the rim of Crater Lake. To the other side we could see all that we had just hiked and climbed over. This was one of my favorite parts of hiking, to be able to stand on high ground and take in what was accomplished for the day.

Charlie and I would get to a peak or a ridge and I'd say "Oh baby, look at that! We were there! We just DID THAT!" The beauty mixed with the feeling of accomplishment made every climb worth it. I stood there, near our campsite, and stared at the rolling hills and peaks we had passed. The Rogue Valley was slipping farther and farther away, although Mt. Mcloughlin was still in view.

After we laid our gear out in the sun to dry, and set up the rest of camp, I took some time to go over the map. I made it a habit to look at the topo, compare it to what we experienced for the day, and then study the water sources and terrain for the next day. I didn't want to make the mistake of passing a water source ever again! Before too long, the gentleman with the cowboy hat and the foreign accent came into camp and began unloading his gear. Charlie and I looked at each other puzzled.

We had seen him periodically that day, resting in the shade on fallen logs. We didn't converse much with him as we passed him, just a nod or a short hello. Most of the time I was unable to speak, breathless from dragging myself up the trail. Stopping was for acquiring oxygen and adjusting my pack to move the pain, not chit chatting or making new friends.

He introduced himself as Slip N Slide. He was twenty-something, and from Germany. He had started in Campo, at the California/Mexico border on the first of April. This was the beginning of his third month on the trail, and he was alone.
"So, why are you hiking the trail?" He asked me.
My mind went blank, "I don't know," I thought more about it, "to see if I can, I guess. To be out here."
I looked at him puzzled, "Why are you hiking the trail?"
"Well," he started, "That is a sad story."

Slip N Slide stared off into the distance silently for a moment, sitting on the ground with his back against his pack. The warm sun cast orange rays of soft light on his cheeks through the trees. I thought he might have been holding back tears.
He swallowed hard and said, "You see, I had never backpacked before. But, my best friend dreamed of hiking the PCT. He asked me to go with him on this trip. Two weeks after I agreed to go, he passed away. So, here I am." He became silent.

The irritation over me being just a section hiker, along with my wounded ego, slowly dissipated and cowered behind

19

the lump in my throat. The three of us sat silent for a moment.

Here is a young man, who just walked almost eighteen hundred miles, with no previous backpacking experience, to honor a dream that was not even his own. He left his friends, his family, the University, the comforts of home and culture, and threw himself into the wilderness on foreign soil.
"You're a wonderful friend for doing this for him", I finally spit out.

"But," he continued, "I now have something that I need to take care of back home. When I get to Crater Lake, I will be leaving the trail."

The lump in my throat dropped and yanked my heart into my gut. We were only twenty-four miles away from Crater Lake. We would be there soon. I didn't want him to have to quit after coming so far! The thought pained me.

I began to think deeply about the magnitude of what Slip N Slide was doing. I wondered if my best friend would have done this trip for me if I had passed away before I had the chance. Long distance hiking/backpacking takes a certain level of determination, a sense of adventure, and a great deal of perseverance. My best friend certainly has all of these qualities, but factor in the terrain and the little bit of obstacles we had already overcome in such a short time. Would anyone do it for me?

Charlie strung up our tarp between two trees, and hung his hammock. I blew up my air mattress, and laid out my bivy and sleeping bag underneath. I liked our sleeping arrangement. I felt secure with him above me. Every night, he was always within arm's reach. Or tapping distance should he wake me with snoring!

"You are not worried that he will fall on you?" Asked Slip N Slide. I giggled at the thought of it, "No, I feel safer sleeping on the ground with him above me." I felt myself pained by saying, out loud, that I felt safer with him there.
Charlie yanked on the hammock, that he had hung between two small wavering trees, "I hope that holds!" he laughed. One of the trees bent down towards the hammock like it was made of rubber as he clambered into the hammock to test its stability.

After firing up our stoves and boiling water for dinner, Charlie and I sat on a log and Slip N slide remained kicked back against his pack. Somehow the topic of guns came up.

"I do not feel safe around guns. Bad things happen when guns are around!" said Slip N Slide.

My eyes widened and I glanced at Charlie, and then to my gun and holster that was still clipped to the hip belt of my pack. I stood up towards my pack and acted like I was getting something out of a side pocket, moving my handkerchief slightly to cover the exposed grip of my gun. Had he already seen it? I wondered. The last thing I wanted to do was get into a political debate about guns, or scare him. I sat closer to my pack, trying to block Slip N Slide's view of my .38 Special, that was fully loaded with hollow points.

Slip N Slide opened his pack and he pulled out a large bottle of Fireball Whiskey. BOOZE! I was excited, but instantly thought about how hard it was to stay hydrated out here. However, my mouth watered at the sight of it.

"A guy gave this to me on the trail, and he didn't want to carry it. Would you like any?" Slip N Slide offered me the bottle.

"I'll just have a sip," I said politely, making an effort to hide my enthusiasm.

At home I indulged in more than my fair share of wine in the evenings. To the point that it was habitual. My bottle of wine was my evening companion that massaged away stress from the day, and covered up anxieties that I didn't want to address. Before embarking on this hike I had joked with Charlie that I would bring two water bladders. One for water, and one for wine. He didn't think it was very funny. But, part of me was a little worried about being out there without it. I took a small Sip from the Whiskey bottle, and handed it back to Slip N Slide. We all sat around making small talk until the sky began to glow orange and pink with the setting sun. I wandered over to the bluff that looked out towards Crater Lake.

I could see for miles and miles. All I could think about was the journey ahead of me. We would reach Crater Lake in less than two days. Slip N Slide would return to Germany, and Charlie would be returning home. I would be carrying on over three-hundred miles more alone. I returned to our camp site and Slip N Slide offered me the bottle again.

"Ok," I agreed, "Just one more sip," and then I tucked myself into my bivy under Charlie's hammock.

Day seven

Morning came and Slip N Slide was awake and headed for the trail as Charlie and I were still getting camp packed. Charlie and I planned on covering about thirteen miles, and the next day would be an even easier ten miles or so to Mazama Village. After refilling our water we headed out. Water was heavy. At 2.2 pounds per liter, we each carried between eight to eleven extra pounds in our packs. Every time we refilled I would think of the thru-hikers we would meet. They didn't carry as much water as we did. Papa-Ratzi said the rule of thumb was one liter for every five miles of travel. Perhaps I was traumatized over our first few days hiking during the heatwave, and being so dehydrated that I couldn't cry real tears.

In the days prior, on the way to Hyatt Lake, I had been so frustrated with the pain that my pack was causing me. I was stopping every thirty to fifty feet to try to adjust my straps, or lean forward on my trekking poles to get the weight off my shoulders and hips. I felt a fiery explosion in my gut, I leaned over my poles with my head down and tried to yell out "I am SO MAD!" I could hardly get the words out.

My body trembled and I made sounds that meant I should have been sobbing, but my throat seized and it was hard to swallow. My eyes could barely trickle my tears of defeat. Charlie kept getting a bloody nose. We were both in a dark place, and the scary thing was that we were both drinking A LOT of water. Fast forward back to day seven on the trail, when we got to a water supply, we filled all of our reservoirs even though the temperature was mild and the terrain was easier.

As we walked, we tracked Slip N Slide. I pointed out the first set of foot prints to Charlie.
"I think these are his. It looks like he is pushing off hard with his right foot." I crouched down to examine the footprint closer,
"Look how the toes on the right dig deep into the ground. And here is the left foot print. He is leading with his left and pushing off with his right."
Charlie agreed, "His pack does weigh 60lbs!"
Charlie took a mental note of the tread pattern. I would notice the foot prints leading off the trail now and again. I would scan the area in those places, looking for fallen logs that he might be resting on.

Although we could track him for most of the day, we never saw him. It was a fun way to pass the time. Searching for the elusive thru-hiker.

I was also noticing a track that I hadn't seen on previous days. Snake tracks. Charlie doesn't appreciate snakes, and because I was in front, I decided I wouldn't say anything about the tracks but be on the lookout (though I am sure he had seen them without my mentioning). It wasn't long before something caught my eye, and my foot was almost on top of it.

"CHARLIE! Where is the camera?" I shouted back to him.

"What is it?" Charlie questioned me.

A beautiful two foot snake lay in the trail, with a giant bull frog's back legs hanging out of its gaping jaws. Charlie dug my phone out of the top of my pack so I could get a picture of it.

"I was wondering if we would see it," I said as I got close to get the pictures, "Beautiful!"

When we got to our prospective campsite, Slip N Slide was already there, kicked back against his backpack on the ground. Charlie scouted around, looking for two trees to hang his bed.

Charlie walked over to Slip N Slide and said, "Are you going to camp there? It would be the perfect spot for my hammock."

Slip N Slide got up, and plopped down in another flat area farther away from us.

After stealing the camp spot Slip N Slide had picked out, Charlie said to him, "Let me see the bottom of your shoe."

Slip N slide looked at him bewildered. Charlie picked up a stick and began to draw a tread pattern in the dirt. Slip N Slide sat back down on the ground and lifted his boot so we could see the bottom of it. It was a perfect match! Slip N Slide looked amused and I laughed.

"Told you we were trackers", Charlie said with a smirk.

Slip N Slide was making camp, after generously letting us have his first choice area because it had more room and trees for our hammock set up. I walked over and sat on a nearby rock, with a handful of Jerky, dehydrated coconut, and my electronic cigarette. He turned to me and chuckled.

"I don't know how you can smoke that out here!" he said.

"It is not really smoking!" I laughed, trying to defended myself.

"Such luxuries you section hikers have!" he joked.

"Hey, I'm not the one with the sixty pound pack, and I still get to keep my luxuries" I joked back.

"Yeah, but it is funny to see, you pull it out every time you stop!" He rebutted.

We sat together and I watched Charlie. He was busy setting up the tarp between two trees.

"What are you going to do without him?" Slip N Slide questioned me, "He always sets up, and you watch him".

My heart sank a little. I had only set up the tarp once, and it was while at home in the backyard on the day I bought it, a few weeks ago. I knew Slip N Slide was on to something, and I had already been worrying about it. Charlie was doing most of the work for us both so far. And I was letting him.

"When he is gone, I will have to set it up differently, using my trekking poles," I replied, still watching Charlie working alone, "I can do it." But it felt more like I was only trying to convince myself that I could.

The three of us gathered around on the ground with our freeze dried dinners. Charlie and I poured boiling water into our Mountain House pouches, and Slip N Slide prepared ramen in a freezer bag. I puffed on my electronic cigarette while I waited for my chicken and rice to hydrate.

Slip N Slide smiled and said "I think that your name should be Smokey. Because you are always smoking on that thing".

I laughed and shook my head. All I could think of was a man with bong stuck to his lips.

Day eight

The next morning Charlie came over to me while I packed up my sleeping bag. It was my least favorite chore. Getting my sleeping bag compressed into the dry sack small enough to fit into the lower compartment of my pack was no easy task.

"I thought of another name for you," Charlie said, "Two Sips!"

Charlie turned on his iPod and played "Patient Love" by Passenger. The line came on, "Got two sips of whiskey in the flask but I'm not gonna drink it, I swear I'll make it last till we're...drinking out of the same glass again..."

I loved that song, and Charlie had been listening to it as we fell asleep the night before; thinking about how we would be apart soon.

"Plus," he added, "you did only take TWO SIPS of whiskey the other night!" I could tell he was impressed with my new restraint.

"Hmmm..." I thought about it.

Slip N Slide chimed in, "Smokey Two Sips!" he said, combining the two names.

"Then, Smokey Two-Sips, it is! I giggled.

2. ALONE

Being the last born of nine children meant that most of my brothers and sisters had created their own adult lives by the time I came around. And most of them, if not all of them, found themselves on babysitting duty at one time or another when my mother had to work or keep other appointments.

One of my sisters had a small apartment in our equally small hometown of Cave Junction. She lived there raising her very young daughter for the time being. I remember a time that I was staying with her for the day. My niece, who was only a few years younger than me, eagerly attempted to join me in play.
"Go away!" I yelled at her, and pushed her.
Her bowed and wobbly toddler legs collapsed beneath her, and she fell onto the deteriorating milk chocolate brown carpet, with a shriek. My sister came running in as my niece started to cry.
"What happened?" She demanded.
"I want to play alone!" I declared.
"Oh yeah?" My sister obviously didn't take my side in the matter, "Then go play alone!"
She sent me to her bedroom without any of my toys, and I laid on the bed, crying...Alone. Just as I had asked.

It was going to be a short, easy, day to Crater Lake. At this point I had decided anything less than fifteen miles was a walk in the park, regardless of elevation gains or falls. I started measuring distance by time. Every two miles was about one hour, including short breaks. We had thirteen miles to go before we could set up camp and pick up my resupply package at Mazama Village. Which meant if we left by 8AM, we would reach the destination by 3 or 3:30PM. Perfect timing for a hot meal, and a hot shower. It had been three days since my last real shower! Record breaking, or so I thought at the time!

Slip N Slide left camp that morning ahead of us, as usual. It was still cool out, so I left my base layers on under my hiking clothes. My hiking clothes consisted of a pair of champion brand nylon basketball shorts and my "Thighs on Fleek" cotton T-shirt.

As we walked, Slip N Slide would appear here and there on fallen logs next to the trail as he always had, twirling one trekking pole in his hand. He would shoot ahead of us with thru-hiker full steam, and then wait for us to catch up. There were many fallen logs to be found, most of them fallen across the trail. My 5'4" frame would stretch across the logs in an effort to clamber over them. Slip N Slide offered a hand to help me over.

I objected gracefully over my tired brow, "Thank you, but at some point I am going to have to crawl over these by myself!"

Slip N Slide got a head of us and climbed up on another log to let us catch up. As we got a little closer, I took a moment to shed my base layers, shielded by Charlie.

We caught back up to Slip N Slid and he asked, "Can I ask you a personal question?"

I daringly nodded my head to say yes...I couldn't imagine what he could possibly ask me out here that I wouldn't want to answer.

"Do you have another shirt you can wear?" He asked, looking me over and glancing at Charlie. I looked at him puzzled.

He continued, "I think that shirt might make some thru-hikers crazy after months of being on the trail without a woman's contact."

I glanced down at my V-neck T-shirt. My cleavage partially exposed, and my breasts were snuggly squeezed behind the chest strap of my pack.

"Yeah, I do. Good point", I chuckled and made a mental note to change into my button up shirt when we got into camp.

The path to Crater Lake quickly turned from flat and easy to burnout city. The forest around us disappeared and transformed into a

27

large burnout with fallen trees and a hard to find trail. No shade, and no birds. Not much of anything but burnt, grey, dying wood. Charlie and I lost the trail while trying to maneuver around the burnt fallen logs, but eventually got back on course.

Slip N Slide was nowhere to be found. After the burnout we found ourselves at a trail junction that was not well marked with the usual trail blazes. I sat down and pulled out the map.
"This is what I would do without you here." I said to Charlie.

In less than 24 hours I would be without him, and I had depended heavily on his confirmation and the teamwork that he had provided. I was sure Charlie already had a plan mapped out in his head of which trail we should take, but he let me try to figure it out.
I pointed to the right and said "I'd go this way!"
Charlie nodded his head in agreement and said "I like it."

We took the trail to the right, and soon met back up with Slip N Slide.

Once we made it to the Crater Lake National Park and trail-head parking area, we stopped to read the trail-head sign and park map.

Written in large letters on the map, "HITCH HIKING IS PROHIBITED WITHIN THE PARK." This meant we would have another mile to walk, and it would be on the paved road. I didn't mind road walking much, but it was harder on the shins and hips after being in the woods. We kept walking on the road until the "Mazama Village" Sign was in view. Less than a quarter mile and one more wake up, Then Charlie would be departing.

As we approached Charlie's final destination on the trail, my memories drifted back a couple years, to when I was dreaming about being on the PCT for the first time.

"You aren't allowed to go," I had told Charlie after explaining to him that I wanted to walk four-hundred thirty miles across Oregon. He looked at me with hurt in his eyes.
"If you go with me, you will end up doing everything for me, and I will let you! I have to do it alone!"
I swore to myself then, that after being "the baby" of the family, this trip was going to teach me to do things for myself. I certainly wasn't going to let a man or anyone else walk this walk for me! Something

inside of me wanted to be broken down, and I wanted to be the one to fix it.

A part of me froze as we approached Mazama Village! My legs were still walking, and we were getting closer and closer, but inside I was yelling at myself. Pleading. Begging not to go a step further. "You know that If you leave here, you leave without him?"

When we arrived at Mazama Village Slip N Slide was eager to get a hearty meal. Charlie and I were eager to shower and set up camp. Even though the thought of devouring a cheeseburger delighted me, I figured it might taste better if I didn't smell like I hadn't showered in three days. And although we weren't technically hiking together, Slip N Slide went along with our plan.

Slip N Slide caught a glimpse of my razor in my toiletry bag. "You're telling me you brought something to make you hairless out here?" He laughed.
"Listen, I might get a little stinky, but no way am I running around anywhere with hairy arm pits!" and I waved my razor at him; which Charlie had cut the handle in half for me before we left, to save weight.

We made our way to the restaurant near the Mazama general store. I passed the salad bar on the way to our table, and my mouth watered. I'm not sure that the sight of fresh spinach and cherry tomatoes had ever made me salivate before, but I suddenly had big plans for that salad bar!

I ordered a bacon cheeseburger, sweet potato fries, one trip through the salad bar, and a beer. Slip N Slide ordered a sixteen-inch pepperoni pizza.

The waiter returned after quite some time and told him, "There seems to have been a communication barrier, and the cook made your pizza with all jalapenos. So it is going to be a little longer."

How does one confuse the word pepperoni with jalapeno? The best I could come up with was the "pepper" correlation. This kept my mind distracted from my stomach while we waited for our salad-bar plates to arrive.

Charlie and I gorged ourselves on the salad bar, and then our burgers came. I offered fries to Slip N Slide while he eagerly waited for his pizza. I made it half way through my burger and decided I couldn't possibly take another bite! I was curious to know when the

"Hiker Hunger" would set in. I heard about it all the time on the trail. Hikers raved about not being able to ever eat enough. I got a to-go box and ordered another beer.

After dinner, we went to the general store to pick up my resupply box, and Charlie called his dad to arrange his pickup for the next morning.

"Hey dad, I have another favor to ask you," Charlie said to his dad into the pay phone, "We made a new friend out here, and he needs to leave the trail to go back to Germany. Can we give him a ride back to Medford?"

Charlie's dad of course agreed.

It was all settled. Dad would come around noon, give us a ride to the rim of Crater Lake, and then I would continue on. Charlie hung up the phone, signifying that my fate had been sealed.

We returned to the restaurant to charge my battery pack. Slip N Slide sat down with me while Charlie checked out the gift shop. He stared at me quietly for a few moments.

"So," Slip N Slide inquired, "How do you feel about being out there alone?"

I didn't answer right away. All I could think was how much I wanted Charlie's company out there.

"I don't know," I wasn't really sure about it now, "I'll be OK," I swallowed hard, "I mean, I was always supposed to do this trip alone. It is the plan".

Slip N Slide tapped my leg with his boot, under the table "You're not afraid to be a female alone?"

I wanted to ask him if anyone had ever asked him if he was afraid to be a man on the trail, alone. But I just stared at him in the eyes.

"I'll be OK," I finally answered again.

He tapped my leg again with his boot and grinned at me.

I opened my resupply box back at the hiker campground, and retrieved my dad's ashes from it. My pack felt much heavier now with extra food and the extra pound of father! But nothing was as heavy as when we first started, so I wasn't going to complain! A good 40lbs is light compared to the 50lbs I started with! I handed Charlie the almost empty fuel canister that we had been sharing.

"I need to get more at the store before we head out tomorrow." I said.

"OK, we will stop on our way out in the morning." Charlie agreed and put the fuel canister in his pack.

That evening I laid beneath Charlie's hammock, staring up at him from below. I could hear the other PCT hikers chatting and laughing amongst themselves throughout the Mazama Village PCT hiker camping area. Mr. Clean and Kibbles and Bits were catching up with Slip N Slide, they hadn't seen him since the Sierras. Drake, Thunder Thighs, and Ice Cream all exchanged hiking experiences.

But I just gazed up at Charlie laying in his hammock, taking in as much as I could. I wanted to remember how the evening breeze felt against my face at that very moment, the smell of the dirt, the sound of his sleeping bag rubbing against the hammock fabric as he tried to get situated. Charlie reached down and tapped me on the forehead as I started drifting off.

"Hey," he whispered, "you better zip up your bivy before you fall asleep. Don't want the bugs to get you." he gently urged; as he had every night we had been out here.

Later I awoke to the sound of Charlie snoring. Normally I would tap him or give his hammock a little shove in an effort to stir him and stop the snoring. This time I laid there and listened to him. It was going to be the last time for a long time that I would hear it, "You're going to miss that too!" I told myself.

Day nine

Before I knew it we were puttering up the winding road to the Crater Lake rim in dad's mint condition 1978 VW camper. I giggled to myself at the fact we were traveling in such a fine German built machine with a real-life German in the back. Then I was grateful that such simple things could make me smile. I was hoping I could remain as easily amused on the trail, while alone.

We became normal Crater Lake tourists at the rim. Snapping pictures, and standing in awe at the pristine deep blue water that filled the crater below us. For a moment I forgot that I had a bit of a hike ahead of me. I was anxious though. I had the thought that maybe I should just go home with Charlie. We had a great little adventure together. I could come back another time. I could be done today. We could be snuggled up in our bed together that night, laughing about almost dying of hypothermia, and losing the trail in the burnout area.

31

"Well are you ready to take off?" Charlie asked with a subtle sadness in his eyes.

I laid my forehead against him and closed my eyes. I tried to say yes, and then I tried to nod my head yes when the words wouldn't come out. Tears streamed down my cheeks, and I clenched my eyes as tight as I could. I trembled and Charlie held on to me tightly.

"Hey," He rubbed on my lower back, "it is going to be OK!" Charlie assured me while he wiped my tears and kissed my forehead. I half laughed half cried while I wiped my snot off his shirt.

The four of us started walking down the discovery trail, which follows the rim of Crater Lake. I would take it until it met back up with the PCT after about eleven miles. As the trail started to make a little bit of a climb, Charlie stopped.

"Got your tracker turned on?" he asked.

I checked my tracker, "Yup!"

Charlie's dad gave me a hug and a kiss on the cheek.

"Don't be afraid to shoot anyone!" he said as he put a strong hand on my shoulder.

Slip N Slide gave me a hug, and then I turned to Charlie. I buried my face in his shirt again and held onto him as tightly as I could.

"You're going to be OK out there babe, and I will come get you if you decide you don't want to take one more step!"

Charlie slapped me on the butt as I turned to leave and said "Now get out of here!" He demanded with a smile.

We both laughed but I couldn't look back at him. I started up the hill, and didn't stop until I knew I was out of sight. I was sobbing.

I was going to miss him so much. I was having so much fun on this adventure WITH him. I rounded the corner and looked back. The view caught me off guard. I could see for miles and miles, to Mt. Mcloughlin and beyond.

Words fell out of my mouth, "Oh my god Baby look at th...." But I stopped in mid-sentence. Charlie wasn't there to see it with me. Everything we had just done in the last eight days, I was looking at it all.

Suddenly, it hit me. My stomach dropped, and I quit sobbing. I turned back in the direction I had left from, and screamed down the trail, "CHARLIE!!!!"

I raised my trekking poles and started to run back towards the trailhead, "CHARLIEEEEEE!" I screamed again louder.

The wind was blowing against me, and carried my voice behind me in the wrong direction. I was afraid he wouldn't hear me, and leave. So I blew as hard as I could on my search and rescue whistle. Soon Slip N Slide appeared running up the hill, then Charlie close behind him, and then Charlie's dad. They had heard me! Their faces frozen with sheer terror and worry!

"I'm OK," I yelled out and waved my hands in front of me in an effort to calm them.

"I'm OK," I breathlessly tried to reassure them again, and I hurried over to Charlie.

Charlie's dad stopped at the top of the hill and wiped his forehead with his handkerchief. I felt terrible for causing so much worry!

"Jesus!", Charlie shook his head with relief, "I thought for sure you were dangling from the cliff!"

Slip N Slide came over to us, still looking bewildered about why I was making such a fuss. Hid hands were on his hips, and his breathing labored.

"I forgot to buy fuel at the Mazama store," I explained to Charlie, "I gave you the other one, I don't have any. I'm sorry, but I had to let you know before you left".

I had my InReach satellite tracker, which has texting capabilities, but Charlie would not have cell-phone reception until he got closer to Medford. I knew the Crater Lake lodge didn't carry fuel, and it was a steep five mile walk back down to the Mazama Village; not to mention the walk back up.

Since I was taking the rim trail and bypassing some of the PCT, I was going to be walking a long stretch without any natural water resupply sources. Charlie had planned on leaving me water in a bear box that was located at a PCT trailhead parking lot near the north entrance of the park. Theilson Creek would be my first natural water source from that point, and that was twenty-seven miles away. But fuel wouldn't be available for days, and I couldn't go too long without it. Most of my food needed to be rehydrated.

"Ok, don't worry about the fuel, I will get it to you." Said Charlie.

We said our goodbyes again, and I gave Charlie's dad an extra big hug.

"You really scared us kid!" He scolded me with a smile.

"Sorry dad, I want to be able to eat", I explained apologetically.

I started back up the trail, trying again to keep myself from sobbing, but I continued crying for at least the next hour. As I walked the rim trail I would pass day hikers. I hid my face from them or would turn towards the rim in an effort to hide my swollen eyes, and the clear snot running from my nose.

"Good God Crystal, get yourself together!" I ordered myself. "Big tough-girl thinks she can go out into the wilderness all alone for weeks, and she can't even get three steps away from her family without absolutely losing it?"

I continued harshly. "How do you forget to buy fuel? A rookie mistake! What else are you going to screw up out here? Dumb! Dumb! Dumb! You know, you probably have no business being out here! You have never even gone on a backpacking trip!"
"Grrrr…Shut UP!" I growled to myself.

I looked up at the road that the rim trail traversed. Hoping that maybe I would see Charlie leaving the park and I could flag him down to take me home. Then I saw the "falling rock" sign. I stopped crying, and for a moment the sign made me smile.

"Be on the lookout for Falling Rock!" My dad hollered back to me from the driver's seat of their new 1987 Ford Bronco.
My Mom, Dad, sister Denise, and I were headed to the coast for the day. I looked out the car window and saw a bright yellow road sign that said "FALLING ROCK". I glanced around the sides of the cliffs that seemed to stretch out across the narrow highway we were traveling.
"What does that mean?" I innocently asked my parents, the way any curious six-year-old would. My dad looked at me in the rear view mirror, his eyes smiling. I had taken the bait! He began the story:
"A long time ago this area was full of Natives," his eyes widened, "A white guy came through and fell in love with an Indian princess named Falling-Rock. The two loved each other so much that they ran away so they could be together. The tribe has been looking for her ever since; they put up those signs so everyone could keep a lookout for her."
I listened with amazement, and was sure that was one of the coolest things I had EVER heard! My dad glanced back and smiled at me in the mirror. I diligently spent the next few years scanning the cliffs and river's edge for the princess whenever we went to the coast.

"Thanks Dad." I whispered, standing there awestruck by a   hazard sign, the way no one has ever been awestruck by a hazard sign before. I took a deep breath, "You're right, we better keep moving. We have got to get to camp." I felt a sense of calm come over me. I had my dad with me. I had a mission to complete. I had to get his ashes to Tipsoo peak. Charlie had probably already gotten fuel and would be on his way back to the leave it with the water supply at the bear box near the north entrance.

The Rim trail provided views of Crater Lake like I had never seen. The wild flowers were amazing! The sun was amazing! The wind that danced on the water below was amazing! I was filled with gratitude. However the dark clouds in the distance didn't look quite so amazing. "No, please, no rain tonight. I don't know if I can deal with it tonight!" I pleaded.

I reached the PCT and Rim trail junction after about eleven miles. It was getting colder, and the wind was picking up. Just as I reached the trail marker, rain started to sprinkle down. I dropped my pack, dug out my rain jacket and rain pants, and threw them on over my clothes. I felt silly being so frantic over it, but I did not want to get caught up in a storm like Charlie and I did on the fifth of July. My heart grew heavy again, "You're going to be just fine!" I reassured myself.

I could hear cars passing nearby. The parking area where Charlie planned to leave my water and fuel was close. The sign said "1/4 mile" and in the other direction, my camp site should be about another 1/4 mile. I draped my rain jacket over my pack like a poncho, and made my way to the highway. When my eyes caught a glimpse of the White GMC truck, and my heart leaped! Charlie was there! "Look at you!" Charlie said as he greeted me, as if he hadn't seen me in a week.

We visited for a few minutes, but it looked like the storm was coming in. I needed to get to the campsite and get my shelter up before the storm reached me. We said our goodbyes again, and I darted across the street, and disappeared into the woods; carrying my trekking poles in one hand and a gallon water jug in the other.

By the time I made the short half mile trek to the campsite area it had started to rain a little harder. I quickly began pulling out my tarp and fumbled to get it unrolled and spread out. I had chosen a higher flat area, in hopes that the water wouldn't accumulate around me; just as Charlie had done for us in the last storm. My hands were cold, and I could hear thunder starting to roll above me.

"Please God" I prayed "Please just give me ten minutes to get this tarp up." I tried to slow down, and remember how to correctly set up the tarp.

I loosely staked the sides, and started to adjust the first trekking pole that would be the end poles to the A-frame structure. My tracker beeped, I had an incoming message, "Get under-cover, big storm coming fast", it was from Charlie.

My eyes filled with tears and I started making strange squeaking sounds in my throat, trying to hold back from bursting into tears again, "Do not fucking loose it, do not fucking loose it", I kept repeating to myself trying to keep my wits together. I was terrified that I was about to relive the thunder and hail storm that Charlie and I experienced. But this time, I was counting on myself to get the tarp up and keep myself warm. And I did not yet have faith that I could do it myself!

I pulled tightly on the guy-lines, but they wouldn't tighten down. The trekking poles kept collapsing. I tried to remember all the pointers Charlie had given me the day I set the tarp up at home. There was something special I had to do to the lines and toggles to make them tighten down, but what was it was it? Nothing I was doing was working!

The thunder got louder, and I frantically started wrapping the lines as tight as I could around the stakes. The tarp sagged in the middle, and the trekking poles kept taking turns falling over. "This is bad." I thought, "This is really bad!" I grabbed my tracker and messaged Charlie back, "I can't get the tarp up!" The wind swirled around me, and the forest began to come alive with swaying tree tops.

I needed a plan-B. If the rain started coming down, I wasn't going to have my shelter secured in time. I peered out into the trees and the bushes, scanning for something to hide under. Something caught my eye. It was large and black. I tried focusing, and wiped my eyes. Was it a charred tree? I looked around, desperately. There wasn't any evidence here that suggested a past fire. I took a few steps closer, squinting. My eyes could make out the large rounded figure, about two-hundred feet away. Was it a bear?

It didn't seem to be moving. Was it just staring at me? I decided that it was just a charred tree to calm myself, and then went back under my partially sagging tarp. I removed my gun from its holster, and laid it next to my bivy within reach; just in case the charred tree decided to come investigate me. But then something else caught my eye coming down the trail, Charlie's blue shirt!

I was so happy to see him! Even though part of me felt defeated because he was coming to rescue me. "Your first night out here alone and so far you can't remember to buy fuel OR how set up your tarp right! I scolded myself.

Charlie took a look over my set up, and showed me again how to manipulate the toggles on the guy lines to snug things down.

Having to say goodbye to him wasn't getting any easier, even though I'd done it three times already! I invited him to stay another night, and I would have fully appreciated it but he had left his gear at home. Before he left I led him to the edge of my camp and I scanned through the trees and bushes. I stood there, searching, squinting and stretching my neck side to side

"What are you looking for?" Charlie asked.

"I wanted to show you this, uh, burnt tree," I smirked, "it freaked me out a little, and I thought it was a bear at first!"

I shook my head with disbelief, "But, it is not there now."

Charlie patted me on the back, and looked at me sympathetically. I wasn't sure that he believed me. He stayed for just a short while longer, and then hugged and kissed me goodbye. Holding on to me tightly he reassured me that he was proud of me no matter how far I decided to go in the next three weeks, and he made his way back to the trail.

I quickly returned to the shelter of my tarp, hoping it would hide my tears should he turn to wave, but he didn't look back. I saw him wipe his cheek with the back of his hand before he disappeared, and I cupped my mouth so that he wouldn't hear me crying again.

I took a few deep breaths and started planning out the evening. I made a mental list of priorities: 1. Eat, and 2. Study map. That was all there was to do. I wasn't very hungry, regardless of walking over eleven miles that day. The thought of eating after the emotional roller coaster of the day made my stomach turn. I looked through my food bag, and chose some garlic instant potatoes.

The rain came as I sat under my tarp, and I choked down the thick salty mashers. "Thank you God", I said as I looked at the rain drops sliding down my thin tarp. The water ran down the A-frame structure, down the edges of the dirt walls I had dug up around the tarp, and then out towards the slope of the camp site. It made me smile. Something I built for a purpose was actually working, for its purpose! A small sweet victory!

I said thank you a few more times to God for what did go right that day. I hadn't been the most religious person for quite some time. I hadn't prayed earnestly in years. However, I did ask God for enough time to set up my tarp, and not to try to kill me like he did in the hail storm. Because everything worked out almost according to prayer, I figured I owed some heartfelt gratitude. I might need more help later on! And , there wasn't anyone else to talk to.

"God, if you even really hear me," I felt silly, "thank you for keeping me dry, and thank you so much for an amazing husband, and please keep me safe tonight while that shape shifting tree is running around." I giggled, "Just kidding, I really am grateful, I just don't know how to pray well. I am sure you get that all the time." I concluded.

I sat stirring my lumpy dinner, that wasn't fully re-hydrated. I couldn't eat another bite of potatoes, and I still had half a bag left. I found a place under some trees, about two-hundred feet from my shelter, and dug a hole with my trowel. I buried the potatoes, and then piled rocks on top of the fresh soil. Bears can smell grub worms through thick tree stumps, but CERTAINLY these garlic scented spuds would be masked by six inches of dirt and a few lava rocks.

Shaking my head at how brilliant I wasn't, I returned and tucked myself into my sleeping bag. Before falling asleep I looked over my map and chose my next camp site, 16.2 miles away; near Thielson Creek. I was starting to doze off. I knew I should probably find a spot to hang my food bag, but I didn't want to be out in the rain again. I was warm. I was comfortable. And I fell asleep fast.

3. YOU CAN QUIT TOMORROW

Day ten

I awoke groggy and cold in the morning. The condensation that had accumulated inside my bivy made the waterproof plastic coated nylon fabric stick to my hair and face. It had rained all night, and I kept waking to make sure the water wasn't running underneath me. It was still raining. I laid there, not wanting to move. It was just after five in the morning.

Then suddenly I heard a loud drawn out moan that filled the forest around me. I sat straight up, eyes wide, and I scanned the tree line around me. I heard it again, and then again. I couldn't see anything moving, but it sounded nearby! If it was a bear, what was it being so loud about? I just wanted to get out of there. "You don't need coffee," I told myself as I put away my stove and packed up my gear.

The tarp was sopping wet, and covered in mud and pine needles. I rolled it and stuffed it in its stuff sack anyway. Then I heard the sound of tearing wood, followed by noshing and loud chomping. "Yup, time to go, the burnt tree is back, and it sounds like it could use a big breakfast."

I scanned through the trees as I walked quickly down the trail. After about two minutes of walking, a track caught my eye. I crouched down to investigate it further. It was definitely a set of bear tracks. Still crouched, I scanned a few feet ahead of me I spotted another set of tracks. After about fifteen feet, the tracks disappeared to the left of the trail.

I stood there, waiting patiently, watching for movement in the brush, and listening. Nothing. I moved on, constantly scanning the woods around me, behind me, and the path in front of me. And then, a new track.

"Strange", I thought. "Those are certainly toes. Five of them. But, bears don't have arches like this!"

A big smile spread out across my face. I followed the tracks for another fifty yards at least, and then I realized; someone was walking the PCT barefoot!

"Crazy," I shook my head, "What will they think up next?"

The rain poured down. I set my gaze on the trail directly ahead of me. I tried not to think about the rain and the cold. I hated being wet and cold more than anything else. Charlie and I had big dreams of moving to Alaska or Colorado or any place we could be more secluded, but I was starting to wonder how I would fair. Ironically, the wet and cold I was experiencing was not much compared to what I would have to endure in the remote locations we fantasied about. Maybe a tiny-home in Arizona or Central America would be more up my alley!

The rain began to taper off for a bit, but the air was still cold and heavy with mist. It wasn't long before I was bombarded again with mosquitoes. I put on my head net, and carried on. I was moving fast. Much faster than I had been hiking before. "You might have found your hiking legs!" I cheered myself on.

By 10:30AM I had covered almost ten miles, and was keeping my eye out for the water that I had stashed in the previous weeks.

As the morning went on, I thought more about my son. I missed him. I hadn't spoken to him much since I had begun the hike. While leaving the rim trail the day before, I was able to call him. "You scared the crap out of me, Mom! He scolded.
"I haven't heard from you in four days! He continued.
"I don't really have service out here Cole...I miss you". I started to cry again, but didn't want him to recognize it.

I swallowed hard, "I miss you so much. I'm headed past Crater Lake. Thanks again for helping me leave the water out here! That was a fun day trip with you. I will call you in a few days when I reach Shelter Cove".

"OK mom," he said, "Be safe, I want my mama to come home in one piece!" There was a long silence while I tried to hold my self together. "OK baby, you take care too!" I managed to squeak out, and he ended the call.

A week before the hike, Cole and I parked alongside of Highway 138, and found the trailhead that popped out nearest the North entrance of Crater Lake. Each of us wore a small day pack that contained a gallon of water.

"Why did I have to come with you?" Cole whined.
"Because, you don't want your mother to die of thirst out here," I replied, "Besides, I am going to be all alone when I come through here in a couple weeks, and I want to be able to remember you here with me. Quit complaining and I'll get you ice cream at Union Creek when we go home!"
My fourteen year old son helped me stash the two gallons of water off the trail. It was the closest thing to hiking with me that he'd done in years. He hated hiking. Once when he was eight, I took him to see Tunnel Ridge, on the sterling mine trail system. He complained so much for the first quarter mile that I had to threaten him that we would go further if he didn't stop whining. Other than car camping, he usually turns down my invitations to be with me outdoors.
"In the future, don't do this, it is illegal and it is probably a risk to the animals!" I smirked at him. But I knew he would probably never be doing something like this, willingly, ever again. Not for himself anyway.
I camouflaged the gallon jugs behind some large bark strips. We practically ran back down the trail, being eaten alive by the largest swarms of mosquitoes I had ever seen.

I pulled out the gallon jugs from behind the tree bark, and carried them towards the trailhead. I started thinking more about home. About Cole, Charlie, and the struggles we have as a blended family. I quickly halted my thought process. "Nope, you aren't ready for that! Today is not the day you tackle that one. There will be time for that later!" I

41

coaxed myself into thinking about something else, but as I approached the highway a white Vehicle caught my eye, and I backed up a few feet. It was a forest service ranger.

"Crap! They really do check for water stashes!" I thought to myself.

I set the jugs down behind a log, and came back out to the trailhead. The vehicle was parked on the other side, on the other side of Highway 138 near the opposite trailhead. I didn't want them to see me with the jugs. I am a firm believer in LNT (Leave No Trace) ethics; but I am also a firm believer in staying hydrated. I didn't feel I had a choice since there was almost seventeen miles between my last water supply and my next. At the time of the water stashing, I didn't know about the bear box located in the park. I decided I would have breakfast on the side of the highway, and wait for the ranger to leave before bringing the water jugs back out into the open.

As fate would have it, the rain started to pour down right when I began to eat my peanut butter. My food bag was laying out next to my gaping pack. "Not a fast learner, are we" I sneered to myself. I quickly stuffed everything back in my pack and then unrolled my large garbage bag. I scurried under some low tree limbs, dragging my pack behind me.

There was just enough room to sit up right, but the rain poured through the branches. I slung the plastic garbage bag onto the branches above me, making myself a roof. "How is that for fast thinking?" I sneered back to myself. The rain came down harder. Semi-trucks and cars whizzed down the highway through the wall of rain.

The ranger finally emerged from the woods, got in her vehicle, and drove off. It felt like I had been sitting there forever. After sitting for almost forty-five minutes the rain tapered off a little, and I refilled my water from one of the jugs. It was time to go.

"On the move!" I messaged Charlie from my tracker.

I had promised him if I had to stop for more than thirty minutes I would message him, and let him know why. Neither of us wanted to have to alert Search and Rescue without good reason, and if my bleep stopped for too long, it might cause Charlie to think that something wasn't right.

I had made it to Mt. Thielson Wilderness by 1pm. The forest was thick, and the trail climbed steadily up towards the rock face of Mt. Thielson. The higher I got, the colder I got. I tucked my hands on the inside of my rain jacket, which was now soaked through in the sleeves. Mental note: get a better rain jacket.

The up-slope of the trail seemed to keep my mind off of the weather for a while. For almost six-hundred feet I went up, stopping often to catch my breath, and then I crested a saddle. Excitedly I looked sharply to my right. Unfortunately, Mt. Thielson was hiding behind a thick layer of fog. I looked out into the wide open space beyond the saddle; more fog filled the valley below. I sat on a large rock, and snacked on dehydrated fruit. My first climb without a view. The wind picked up, and I was getting colder the longer I sat.

I walked for another hour, downhill, before reaching my planned campsite. It was cold and foggy, but it wasn't really raining too much. I quickly unloaded my gear, and started to make camp. The moment I unrolled my tarp, a heavy sense of self-doubt took over. "Slow down. Don't panic!" I repeated my brother's words of wisdom to calm myself.

My hands were cold and wet, and the freezing wind was blowing up the hill. I got the lines staked in, and snugged them down a little, just like Charlie had showed me. I put the trekking poles in place, and raised the A-frame. It was standing, but it sagged deeply in the middle. I decided to adjust the guy-lines and try to get it tighter, but one trekking pole fell over, and the shelter collapsed.

I approached the pole, frustrated, and then I noticed one of the lines had come loose from a stake. I bent over to reattach it, "Where is the stake...?" I moved around in a small circle looking for the stake that the line had been tied to. I gently kicked dirt side to side, hoping to see the shiny metal poking up from the ground. Nothing. The wind blew harder. "Way to go Crystal. Way to freaking GO!"

Again, I was overwhelmed with the thought that maybe I didn't belong out here by myself. I walked away from the shelter and sat down on a nearby log. I messaged Charlie, "I feel so stupid, I can't do tarp. Lost a stake". I had started to sob again, I was so angry at myself.

"You know you can do this... You know you can figure something else out. Why are you letting something so small make you feel so incompetent?" I tried to talk myself down.

" Maybe because it is JUST a tarp and you can't handle even that!" My inner battle was really starting to heat up, but I urged myself to try again.

43

I grabbed the loose line, and tied it to a nearby sapling, using a figure eight knot. For twenty more minutes I made adjustments to the shelter, trying to get it as near perfect as I could, so that it would hold up in the weather.

I stood there looking at the end result, "It is not as good as Charlie could do it, but it is better than what you started with last night." I assured myself that whatever my best was RIGHT NOW, was the best that I had at the moment, and I could only get better.

The rain and wind picked up as I sat under the tarp, eating a dehydrated meal: Chicken and Rice. I tried to focus on my achievements for the day, and make amends with myself for the mistakes I had also made that day. I sat in the darkness, listening to the wind howl up the hill and through my A-frame shelter.

I cried, wishing still that Charlie could be with me. I prayed for sunshine, and I wondered what I would do without the stake I lost. I thought about my son. I thought about all the family time I was missing. I thought seriously about going home.
"Wait and see how you feel tomorrow," I made myself promise. "If you still want to quit tomorrow, you can quit tomorrow."

I turned on my phone, and scrolled through the photos; stopping on the picture I took of a page in the military survival book that my brother had leant to me.

"The assortment of thoughts and emotions you will experience in a survival situation can work for you, or they can work to your downfall. Fear, anxiety, anger, frustration, guilt, depression, and loneliness are all possible reactions to many stressors...When you cannot control these reactions in a healthy way, they can bring you to a standstill... Instead of rallying your internal resources, you listen to your internal fears. These fears will cause you to experience psychological defeat long before you physically succumb... "Survival", US Army manual, 2002

I wasn't in a survival situation such as being lost in the woods, or a prisoner of war. However, mentally surviving on a long distance hike would make or break my physical success; no matter how much gear I had, or time I spent preparing the journey.
"See how you feel tomorrow," I repeated to myself, "You can't decide to quit on a bad day."

Day eleven

The next morning I drug myself out of my bivy. I stopped at Thielson Creek first thing after packing up camp. The rain was still persisting, and the cold wet air made my fingers hurt. I crouched down next to the creek to refill my water bottle, and then filter it into my reservoir. The icy water that ran off the glacier above me tasted like snow. I sat on the bank, staring up towards Mt.Thielson, as the water slowly filtered through my Sawyer Mini.

The peak was concealed, and I could only see spurs of glacier peaking from behind the blanket of fog.
"Hello pretty lady," I said to the mountain.
"I know you're there, I wish I could see you," I smiled.
'Thank you for the water today. It is lovely."

I returned my full reservoir to my pack, and sat quietly for a few moments, still staring towards the peak, hoping to catch a glimpse of the magnificent lighting rod of the cascades. "Another day," I thought as I packed out.

I turned on my tracker, and posted a message, "Starting day, five miles until I spread dad's ashes." I was feeling lonely, but encouraged because I had a mission to complete. A destination. A purpose for the day to keep my mind off of everything else.

The five miles flew by! I was standing at the Oregon/Washington PCT high point before I even took my first break of the day. "This is IT"? I thought as I looked around. The fog settled in around the hill tops. The rain sprinkled down just enough to keep my face and gear wet. I couldn't see Tipsoo peak.

According to the plan, I would leave the trail and climb up to the peak, spread my dad's ashes and then continue on for the day. "This is a dismal, dreary place to leave you..." I thought, to my dad. I sat down on the muddy trail, and ate a Snickers. Charlie had loaded a proposed track into the GPS to help me get up the unmarked side of the hill and back to the PCT.

I looked over my map, sitting there, and looked around me wanting to get eyes on Tipsoo. But, it wasn't visible. Leaving the trail, even with my GPS, meant entering into the fog with limited visibility, and no prior knowledge of what obstacles lay before me. "A lot of our search and rescue missions start out this way", I thought. I messaged Charlie, "Taking dad with me. So wet and foggy don't feel comfortable leaving trail".

I threw on my pack, and started back up the trail, "Let's go dad. I'll find you some where beautiful". Although part of me was disappointed that I was unable to rid my pack of the extra pound!

The day drug on, and all eighteen miles went by without running into a single person. Day two of complete solitude. Day two of walking in the rain. Day three of dreading having to mess with the soaking wet, muddy, and cumbersome tarp.

I arrived at Six Horse Spring, and was surprised to see other hikers! Many of the through hikers we had met at Mazama Village were there refilling water. Drake, Thunder thighs, Ice cream, Mr. Clean, and a few section hikers who didn't yet have trail names. Rumors were flying that Seven was hurting, and might be leaving the trail.

Drake joked he had been trying to catch up to him, and that Seven was probably days ahead of him by now, even with an injury. I sat near the group, mostly quiet, watching the hikers appear and disappear down the steep trail to the horse spring, to refill their water. I had hardly drank much water that day. The cold wet conditions had kept my thirst at bay. In fact, I still had almost three liters in my pack. After a few short conversations and polite hellos, I decided it was time to pick another fight with my tarp.

It was only 4PM, but I was worn out between the miles and the wet weather. My tarp went up and as usual, sagged deeply in the middle. More hikers came up the trail and into the camp area, and I recognized two of them.

"Hey!" I shouted out, accompanied by an obnoxious jazz hand wave.

The two stared at me for a moment, and then replied.

"Oh hey!" and waved back to me.

Charlie and I had met Chris and James on day one, when we were sprawled out in the shade near the "Piped-Spring." They also stopped there for water.

Chis and James had traveled together from Portland to hike the Oregon section as well. We briefly compared a few notes about our hike, and I filled them in on Charlie returning home, and how I got a trail name. They now had a friend who was accompanying them for a three day section. Chris took one look at my tarp and offered to help me with it. As much as I wanted to accept, I turned down the offer. It was hard enough accepting help from my husband. I was out here to do it alone.

I retreated under my sagging tarp and curled up in my sleeping bag and bivy. The rest of the hikers made camp, brewed instant coffee, and shared stories. I just wanted to sleep.

"It would be cool if we had another wind storm like last night!" I heard James say.

I shuttered at the thought

"No it wouldn't!" I hollered from behind my sagging nylon walls.

"Sorry Two-sips, I meant I hope it doesn't storm!" he replied sarcastically, laughing.

I took comfort in having other hikers in camp with me, especially faces that I recognized, even though I had only met them all once before. However, I was still missing home like I never would have believed. I dreaded the thought of having to set up my tarp one more time. In addition to it being hard to set up properly, the wind would rip through it. Condensation built up in my bivy, and I would wake constantly through the night with wet nylon suffocating me.

I wasn't afraid to be out there. I wasn't afraid of animals, people, or camping alone; all the things I thought would get to me first. But my emotions and my thoughts weighed on me heavily. I tried to picture dealing with them for the next 20+ days. The thought made me cry. I felt SO alone! I messaged Charlie from my tracker, "Contemplating where I want u to pick me up missing home." About fifteen minutes later I messaged him again, "Don't send [next resupply] box till I decide at Shelter Cove".

I would be at Shelter Cove in less than two hiking days. It was close enough for Charlie or someone to come pick me up, if that is what I decided to do. I repeated to myself, "Wait until you see how you feel tomorrow. And then decide." Charlie messaged me back, "Awe baby, read the last page in your journal!"

I hadn't even written anything on the last page of my journal! Digging it out of my pack, I opened the small paper book to the last page. Charlie had snuck my journal at one point when we were still hiking together. When I saw Charlie's hand writing I muffled my squeaking sobs with one hand, so the other hikers wouldn't hear me falling apart. It read:

Crystal,

I want you to know how proud I am for you doing this trip. By the time you read this we will have split ways. I miss you and I love you with all I have. I know you got this trip and you will do just fine! I just wish I could be with you. You may be solo but you are not alone. I (along with family and friends) am there with you, rooting you on.
See you at the Bridge of the Gods, my love.
Yours truly,
Charlie

I sat quietly reading and re-reading the note over and over again, sobbing. He knew, long before I did, that at some point I was going to need to be talked into staying. I was going to be lonely. I was going to want to quit. He never wanted me to be out here alone, and he found a way to make me feel like he was by my side every moment. I laid there, clutching my journal, until I fell asleep.

Day twelve

I awoke the next morning around 6AM to the sounds of the thru-hikers packing and hitting the trail. Those that had made their way from the Mexican border were putting in long miles each day. They would hike from sun up to sun down. Their packs weighed 10-15 pounds less than most section hiker packs, and they had already put in over one thousand eight hundred miles at this point. Their bodies were conditioned hiking machines. My body was starting to become angry with me. My hips and calves were stiff when I woke, and my shoulders burned.

Chris, James, and their friend Alfredo were just getting up.
"Are you guys gonna take the skyline trail too?" I asked.
"Yeah, there is more water on that route", Chris replied.

The three men carried a lot of water, and would stop for it every opportunity they had. Most of the alternate routes they had taken over the last couple weeks were routes that offered more water options. The Skyline trail was shorter than the direct PCT route, and it went past some small lakes and ponds. I was lured to it by the luxuries promised at Crescent Lake in the Halfmile notes when I was planning my trip. It reported, "Large campsites, bathrooms, and running water".

I tossed my pack over one shoulder while I supported it with one thigh, then heaved it onto my back; bending forward to cinch my hip belt in place and lock it down. I started down the trail, both of my feet screaming at me. It took about thirty minutes to an hour each day for my body to go numb and relax from the previous day's work. My toes and arches of my feet hurt the worst. They were stiff and tender.

I also had blisters around my toes and the pads of my feet, and I tried my best to care for them. I stopped often to adjust my laces, or change up the lacing pattern to match the terrain (uphill, downhill, rocky, flat) and every evening after taking off my boots I would drain my blisters, wipe them down with antibacterial wipes, and let them breath open to air. I rarely slept with socks on, even when it was cold. My number one priority, much of the day, was taking care of my feet, and making sure my blisters didn't tear open!

It was still raining off and on. I marched on, trying to keep my mind off the cold weather. I started thinking about Charlie's letter any time the weather would start to get to me. I was ashamed of how badly I wanted to quit the day before. For the first time I realized how unprepared psychologically I was for this trip, and how true it was that the mind would convince the body to give up long before the body was ready. I made myself promise that I would not get wrapped up in self-doubt any more. Not just during this trip, but ever again!

I messaged Charlie, "I think I want you to send me a small tent". It was hard to send the message. I didn't want to ask for any help. But, it was better than asking for a ride home! Even still, I wanted to live with my choices, and somehow asking for a new shelter felt similar to cheating or giving up. But, a new tent meant less dread, more rest, and a more positive attitude.

"I'll go look into it today bb. Stay tough love!" Charlie replied, almost immediately.

Within the hour Charlie was at REI setting up tents, searching store inventory, and asking me questions about what I preferred. By 11AM Charlie sent me another message, "You'll have a tent in shelter cove bb. Keep kicking ass. SO many here proud of you".

I raised my head to the sky, and blinked threw the occasional rain drop, "Thank you God for an amazing husband!"

The sun came out long enough for me to eat lunch. But the rain picked up with a vengeance by the time I reached the Skyline Trail. Thunder began to roll above me. I quickly ran for a nearby tree that was still dry underneath. It poured down for a few minutes, and I came out from under the shelter of the tree when it stopped.

Within five minutes, the thunder crashed again, and the rain came back; I flew back under the first tree that could provide cover. Moving on again, I began to pay attention to the birds. I noticed each time, just before the rain, they would all swoop into the tree limbs and become silent. I watched and listened.

The birds sang, and played gingerly in wet tree tops when there was little to no rain. Suddenly, they would fly up and then dart for cover and stop singing. I followed suit, tucking myself and my gear under another tree. CRASH! The thunder clapped and the rain poured down. I sat and waited, not for the rain to settle down but for the birds to start singing again. When the birds returned to chirping and playing, that is when I would move out. I repeated this cycle successfully four or five more times, before the storm passed; a sort of dance with the natural world.

Soon I ended up on a paved road. Reviewing my map, I couldn't find any place that the trail intersected with a road of any kind. I could see Crescent Lake in the near distance, and decided I would walk the road the rest of the way. After a couple of miles I reached the campground, and I had hopes of running into more PCT hikers. Many of them had said they were taking this route, but it was a huge camp area, and there was no one in sight except for the RV campers along the lake in the far off distance.

I cut through the empty campsites, and made my way towards the lake where the RV campers and weekenders accumulated. I walked and searched for a place to call home for the night, but before I could find the perfect spot it started to rain again, HARD! As I ran to the nearest camp site, my pack bouncing and clanging behind me, I heard the sounds of mothers calling their children and watched campers run into their RV's closing the doors behind them. I unraveled my tarp and scrambled to get the stakes out of the bag. CRASH! More thunder! Hail began to sting my cheeks, and the rain soaked my hair. I needed shelter!

I dove under the picnic table and pulled my pack in as close as I could. There wasn't room for both of us. My tarp was laid out on the picnic table-top above me. I just sat there. I looked up, starring at the spider webs and nest eggs, chewed bubble gum, and unidentifiable nasty things stuck to the underside of the table. My rain pants were now covered in a mix of ashy dirt and rain water. At least a half of an hour had passed and the rain continued to pour down. Soon, flooding water started to trickle under the table. I used my hands to build up walls with the dirt, trying desperately to keep the water out.

"This Fucking sucks!" I thought to myself.

Just then Charlie's best friend Gabe messaged me on my tracker. He and his wife were following my journey online via an online InReach account.

"Lisa and I are thinking of you! Keep your head up you can do this." The message said. I took a deep breath and read the message a few times to clear my mind.

When the rain stopped, I stayed for a few moments under the table. I was afraid to even try to set up my tarp. For the moment I was at least under some sort of shelter! After a while the campers flooded out of their RVs, and I could hear sounds of kids laughing. A couple on bikes zoomed past the campsite, and a girl walked past with her dog. Everyone looked so happy. So carefree. I watched them all, like a fly on the wall. I started to cry.

"I would love to see my family", I thought, "but no! I am sitting under a damn picnic table, covered in ash, and I have to set up that STUPID tarp!"

I went from sad to angry, and pulled myself out from under the table. I stomped on the stakes with resentment as I made an attempt at raising my tarp. I wasn't angry that I was alone, or without my family. I was angry because in reality, the close bond that used to hold our small blended family together had been slowly dissipating over the last few years.

I started thinking again of Charlie and Cole. Soon I was thinking of their relationship, and their struggles. Our struggles. I became angrier, more heart broken, more violent with my tarp. I wasn't trying to control my thoughts or save them for later. I started to sob harder than in the previous days. I didn't care who could hear me, or what anyone thought.

"You know, even if Cole and Charlie were both here, we wouldn't be having a great time." I vented to myself, "Someone's feelings would be hurt! Someone would be irritated! No one would be laughing…"

I was bent over my tarp, cursing and sobbing, when my fierce outburst was interrupted and I heard someone say, "Two-sips?"

I looked up startled, and quickly wiped the clear snot that was hanging from my nose. It was Chris! He stood there, looking confused and deeply concerned. I didn't bother with greeting him, although I was happy to see him!

"Are you guys camping nearby?" I blurted out

"Yeah!" He replied.

"Oh my god, can I stay with you?" I practically begged.

"Of course", He seemed surprised

" I thought it was you over here. I don't know anyone else with this damn green tarp," he laughed.

    I stuffed what gear I could into my pack, and in a hurry. Chris grabbed my tarp and balled it up in his arms. At first I thought I should be the one to carry it. "Screw it", I told myself "let the man help you!"

    With my tarp rolled into a wet muddy ball, Chris led me to where he, James, and Alfredo were camped. Alfredo made me a cup of Starbucks instant coffee, and Chris built a fire. The storm had passed by, and rays of sun shined through the trees. We laughed and made jokes as we ate our dehydrated meals, and drank more hot coffee. The camp host came by, and gave us free fire wood so we could warm up by a fire. After we all get settled in around the campfire, Chris spoke up.

"You know, Two-sips", he said with a big smile, "When I found you back there... I just want to let you know...that was the most pathetic display of despair I have ever seen!" He joked and laughed.

    All I could do was laugh at his comment and shake my head. He had no idea how pathetic I really did feel.

4. HOPE

Day thirteen

It had rained all night. I woke several times to check the sand wall I had built up around my tarp, and make sure the water was being redirected away as it ran down the A-frame sides of my tarp. But by morning the sun was shining, and the sounds of birds chirping greeted me just after 5AM.

I laid in my bivy and sang to myself, "Rise up this mornin', smile with the risin' sun, three little birds...by my doorstep...singing' sweet songs. Of melodies pure and true...singing... this is my message to you..." Bob Marley had been stuck in my head for much of the trip. "sayin' don't worry...bout a thing...cause every little thing...gonna be alright..." It seemed to be a fitting anthem for my journey so far. Maybe that or the Crybaby theme song!

I stretched my stiff legs and pointed my toes, rolling my ankles around. Clambering out from under my tarp, I could hear the guys each rustling around in their own tents. I stood there in the sun, with my chin up, arms out stretched, and eyes closed, soaking in the warm rays. "Thank you sun!" I whispered. Diamond peak lit up in the sun light, and the water of Crescent Lake steamed in the morning glow.

Chris and Alfredo began to break down their gear, and I set a few of my things in the sun to dry out before packing them. James was still in his tent, and hadn't made much of a sound when suddenly he yelled out from behind his tent walls.

"Are the biscuits and gravy ready?" Laughter filled the campsite. James joined us at the table for oatmeal and coffee. He pulled off his sock to inspect his blister. I had heard about it, but I hadn't seen it yet. I peeked around to see the bottom of his foot, rested on his knee.

"Oh my dear god," I belted out, almost cowering in fear.

The entire bottom of his foot was covered in one huge blister that spanned from the pad below his toes to heel of his foot. It was flat, almost flush with the shape of his foot. When he pressed on it, a yellow milky substance bubbled under the calloused skin.

"Dear lord, you need to drain that!" I cried out, and offered James a needle and antibacterial wipes, but he declined.

"I'll throw some mole skin on it, it looks better than it did," he winced as he wiped it down and changed the mole skin.

I felt bad for complaining about the blisters that were starting to cover my pinkie toe, and the random few I had on the pads of my feet. I couldn't help but stare until he put it away.

"Hey," it occurred to me, "you all met that guy that was barefoot back at horse springs, right?"

The day I made it to six horse springs, I laid under my tarp quietly trying to talk myself out of quitting and too tired to converse with my fellow hikers, when I saw a set of bare feet walk up the trail. I assumed it was the guy I had been tracking after leaving my first camp after Crater Lake, but lost sight of his prints.

"Yeah," James responded, "He's thru-hiking barefoot. That's his name, Barefoot!" James explained.

"He has a pair of shoes he puts on occasionally, and he is carrying his grandfather's old backpack."

I thought about how people were setting speed records, and south bounding during the winter, and all the other ways people were trying to one up each other out here; trying to one up themselves. People are definitely hiking their own hikes, but it is getting more complicated for people to just come out and hike! Next year maybe I can be the first woman to hike it while wearing a Sasquatch suit, and riding a uni-cycle.

Around 8:45AM we loaded up and headed back for the road. We would have a two mile road walk before getting to a horse camp, and then another mile or so before reaching the trail intersection to make our way to Shelter Cove. This was the latest start since I had started the trip, but I was really happy to be walking with a group of new friends. Being alone had started to take its toll on me after three days. It doesn't sound like a long time, but after a while, you start thinking of the things you never had time to think about before.

Out here, there were no distractions, nothing to keep your mind off the things you'd rather ignore. Sometimes, the distraction of someone else's chatter drowned out all the other thoughts that were trying to surface. But, time after time the guys flew ahead of me. One thing I knew was true: I could hike for 10-12 hours a day, but I was not fast!

I caught up to them every so often when they stopped for a snack or stopped to treat James' blisters. Even though they were moving faster than me, the day was taking longer because they were taking quite a few breaks.

Charlie messaged me, "Everything ok? Don't seem to be covering much ground today?"

"Yeah," I responded, "James has bad blisters, taking it slow with the group. I like the company."

Even though it was only twelve miles to Shelter Cove, we didn't arrive until around 4PM. That meant we had traveled less than two miles an hour over the day. But, I was more concerned with getting a soda, chips, and a beer. I dropped my pack in the covered hiker area. The resort provided an area for PCT hikers to "explode" their packs, go through resupply boxes, and hang out.

There were a lot of hikers already there. Many of them I hadn't met yet. I dug my debit card out of my pack and went inside to pick up my resupply box, and snacks. I came out with my box, a large bag of cheddar cheese Ruffles, a Mike's Hard Lemonade, and a Pepsi. "So when does hiker hunger set in?" I asked another hiker, who was eating a whole pizza himself.

"It is different for everyone." he said.

"I don't ever feel that hungry. I am just excited to have something other than what I have been carrying." I said.

I took a swig of the Mikes, and opened the bag of chips. The salty taste of the chips triggered something primitive, and I moved away from the table so I didn't scare the other hikers. After a few minutes the bag was empty. The beer and soda were gone, and I was making my way back into the store. This time I returned with a 12-inch pizza, a real beer, and a package of cream filled cookies.

"I think I found my hiker hunger!" I laughed, as I passed by the hiker.

I plugged my phone in to a power strip that the resort put out for the hikers. I was anxious to talk to Charlie and Cole, and post some pictures on Facebook to update my friends. I hadn't had internet access since the day I left Crater Lake, and even then I couldn't really post anything. I thought about how strange it was to be so dependent on plugging in.

After my few days alone I was glad to be talking to real people. I wasn't normally glad to talk to people in person back home. Especially people I didn't really know. But, I could scroll through Facebook for hours all week, text, and watch TV... But I dreaded being around people at the store, meeting new people at gatherings, and just putting myself out there in general; it made me anxious. But out here, I jumped right in, I greeted other hikers as if I had known them for years, even though they were all strangers.

Maybe it was the common ground we shared, the trail. We were all some sort of crazy for being out here. Wandering in the same direction, all of us looking for something we couldn't find back home, and most of us didn't know what that was yet. Perhaps it is like that in real life too, and most of us just don't get that. Except, instead of the being on the trail you're standing in line at the grocery store together, or stuck in the same lane of traffic, or are working in the same office building.

While I waited for my phone to charge I messaged Charlie from the tracker, "made it, got resupply box."

He wrote back, "Nice Job bb. Save box so can send tarp and bivy back."

A new sense of calm came over me. The sun was shining, my husband had come to the rescue and the tent was on its way. Somehow I felt OK about setting up my tarp one last time.

"I can do anything once." I thought.

I had spent two days wanting to give up and I didn't, I had made new friends, and I had an incredible hiker appetite. After two weeks I finally felt like I could be out here and do this. I sat by the water and watched the sunlight dance on Odelle Lake, "sayin' don't worry...bout a thing. Cause every little thing...gonna be alright..." I hummed to myself, sitting near the dock.

The store at Shelter Cove was closed by six in the evening. I was disappointed because another beer and a handful of Laffy-Taffy candy sounded like heaven. I could live without the snacks and cold beverage. What I wanted most though was the ability to call Charlie and my son Cole. However, only Wi-Fi was available, no cell service. I had been looking forward to hearing their voices after not being able to talk to them for so many days.

With a heavy heart, I sat at the hiker table for a couple more hours, only leaving to set up camp or sit by the lake. I had a lot that I could be doing, like showering and doing laundry. But, sitting seemed to take priority over moving.

"You haven't showered in five days Crystal!" I scolded myself. "What is one more?" I convinced myself.

My shirt smelled of dusty dirt mixed with BO. I hadn't packed deodorant because it was more that I would have to carry. Albeit small, I was living by the fact that ounces equal pounds, and pounds equal pain; deodorant would be pointless weight to carry. Besides, there isn't a deodorant that can combat the level of physical activity I was up against every day. I was going to sweat, I was going to stink, and I was OK with that (until I had to crawl into my sleeping bag with myself)

It was amazing to watch the hikers, and listen to their stories. Some thru-hikers, some section hikers. I was doing it. I was one of them. I was living my dream. This was an experience I had dreamed of, planned for, and implemented. I sat and soaked in every face, every back pack, every smell, and every bit of the world around me.

We wore the same painful looks, and all hobbled with the same "hiker hobble" around the resort. But, we glowed with a certain sense of freedom that you don't see in people in the day to day grind. For years I had felt awkward around other people, and had never really felt like I fit the mold. However, I am a great actress, and most of the time I can hide my social anxiety. But here, around these people, I felt like I fit right in.

Weekend campers and tourists approached the table. I noticed how clean they all looked. I could smell laundry detergent and shampooed hair in their passing. They would stop sometimes, asking questions and wanting to know details of everyone's journey

"How do you get your food?"

"How long have you been out here?"

"How long will it take?"

"What do you do about water?"

"What have you learned?"

It was amazing to see so much interest be followed with, "Oh I could never do that…"

They met me with even more shock and disbelief when they found out I was out there alone. They told me I was brave and courageous, but I never could quite swallow that. I didn't feel like I was doing anything more than what anyone else could do. I felt like if I could do it, then anyone could!

In fact, there were many hikers out there alone, and I wasn't the only female by myself. It saddened me to hear people say how much they would love to do what we all were doing, hiking the trail, but then immediately dismiss their wonder with the insinuation that they were far too incapable. I wondered if they had even tried it. This was my first backpacking trip, and look how far I had come. "You need to help change that." I told myself.

The sun started to go down, and it began to get very cold. I retreated to the campsite that I was sharing with Chris and James. We had only been hiking together for the last day, but they were becoming dear to me. It made me sad to know that they would be moving on in the morning, and I wasn't sure if I would ever see them again. I would be staying behind to wait for my new tent.

It was ok though. I knew I would be ok on my own. But, I was going to miss their crazy funny jokes and laughter. They certainly made things a little brighter! After a cup of hot chocolate and a dehydrated meal, I tucked into my bivy for what I knew would be my last time. Ironically enough the tarp went up easily compared to the last few nights, and it didn't sag so low in the middle one bit.

But, the tent was in the mail and I was done with the wet, dirty mess and the suffocating bivy. Bits of mud and wet pine needles clung to the underside of the lime green nylon fabric. I watched the water droplets slide down the sides. I closed my eyes and listened to Chris and James joke about not being able to pee outside of their tents because we were all camping so close to each other, not to mention the girl in camp.

Out of all of the people in the world, these guys fell into mine, and they were a perfect fit. Even if I never saw them again after tomorrow, I would certainly remember the laughs for a life time. "Well," I thought "at least they are decent humans!" I laughed to myself.

"Better zip up Crystal...don't want the bugs to get you" I said to myself and I whispered goodnight to Charlie and Cole in my mind, before falling asleep.

Day fourteen

I awoke to my stomach aching and groaning. This was the first time I had woken with extreme hunger. It was 5AM, almost my normal breakfast time. I tried to make myself fall back asleep. I hadn't slept past 5AM in quite some time. My body was getting accustomed to waking with the sun, breaking camp, and pushing on by 7AM.

The thought of drifting back off to sleep sounded heavenly. But, I began to get anxious laying around and at 5:45 made my way to the hiker area to plug in my battery pack and phone. The store didn't open for a little while longer, so I decided to open my resupply box and reorganize my pack. I would save the box, and use it to ship my tarp and bivy back home.

Chris and James were up and ready to move on by 8AM. "You and Charlie are always welcome if you're ever in Portland," said Chris.

"Yeah, you guys too. I mean, if you're ever in Medford." I extended the invitation.

Chris and James both busted up laughing.

"Yeah, Maybe if we are passing through", added James.

We all laughed. Medford is a large city, and still growing, but the need to be there is minimal. Day dreaming of living elsewhere is a regular occurrence for me.

As I walked into the store, I was hit hard by the smell of hot food and espresso. Most of the food available was microwavable food that needed to be pulled from the freezer and paid for before the clerk would throw it in the microwave for you. But there was a hot roller full of breakfast sausage and hot dogs, and the espresso menu must have listed over one-hundred different flavor combinations.

I ordered a German sausage dog with sauerkraut, and a cinnamon mocha. As I paid for my food my mouth watered, and I dug out some extra cash.

"How much do the showers cost?" I asked.

"$1.50 for three minutes." the woman at the front desk replied.

"Can I get $10 in quarters please?"

The woman handed me the roll of quarters, and then I remembered the box I needed to ship back.

"When does the UPS truck usually get here, I am expecting a shipment today, and I have a box to send out."

"No later than 6PM," She said, "but, uhh, we don't ship out packages!"

I stood there for a moment in disbelief. I had a lot of expensive gear to get back home. I certainly didn't want to just leave it behind in the hiker box! I turned and left the store without saying a word, shocked.

I took my food outside and sat in the sun, gorging myself on what I would have crowned the best damn sausage dog in the history of time.

I messaged Charlie, "Problem, this place doesn't ship out packages!"

After breakfast I went back to the campsite and gathered my laundry and my toiletry bag. Laundry was going to cost me about $3. That meant I would have enough quarters to take fourteen minute shower. The shower facility was pretty nice. There were two separate stalls, side by side in one out building.

The showers were clean. And even though each stall was fairly private, I locked the main door behind me. I wanted to be sure I got my money's worth of warm water, so I fully undressed before putting in the first round of quarters, $1.50. The hot water shot out of the shower head, and the water running down my legs quickly turned from clear to grayish black streaks, and pooled on the shower floor around my feet.

My waistline was shrinking after two weeks of steady hiking and the skin around my belly button wrinkled. I had been losing weight fast enough that my skin couldn't keep up. The day I had given birth to my son, almost fifteen years ago, I remembered looking at myself in the mirror, horrified at the sight of my stretched out belly; it resembled what I would imagine Yoda's belly would look like. This was a close comparison. Yoda shower scene, not hot! I giggled.

I began to wash my hair, and as I ran my fingers through the waxy strands. Large clumps of hair fell through my fingertips.

"Well, that's a good excuse to have a second breakfast!" I assured myself.

I was starting to wonder if a multivitamin should have been on my packing list. I continued to load quarters into the money slot, even though I was done washing. "Take that California!" I thought smugly to myself. When I figured I had just enough left to do laundry, I let my time run out, and got dressed.

After throwing my hiking clothes in the washer, located next to the shower building, I made my way back to the store. I got a handful of Laffy-Taffy, a Pepsi, and a breakfast burrito. A thru-hiker approached the table and handed me a laminated flier.
"It is a number for a local trail angel," he said, "I found it in the hiker box."

I looked over the flier, and it listed all of the services the trail angel could provide. "Rides between road closures, rides to medical services, rides to the airport, etc."

I wondered if this guy could help me get to the nearest post office, which was ten miles away. I didn't have cell service on my phone, so I went inside the store to see if the clerk could help me out. "Do you have a phone I could use?" I asked the woman behind the desk.
"We don't have a public phone, what do you need?" She asked.
I couldn't tell if she seemed concerned or suspicious.
"I have a number for a local trail angel. I need to see if he can help me mail out my package."
The woman began to shake her head no, "We don't allow trail angels in Shelter Cove!" she answered.
"WHAT?" I shouted out in disbelief.

How can that be? I was so confused. It wasn't like I was going to call this person and ask him to come take away all of their business! "Look, I need to talk to him. He would be doing me a favor...providing a service you don't provide to your customers". I pleaded.
"Please... I will meet him off site if I need to."
She looked at me apologetically, "Management says no trail angels, sorry."

I started to tear up, "I have two-hundred dollars worth of gear, and then some to ship home. I can't just LEAVE IT! what do YOU suggest I do?" I snarled while holding back more tears.

It was no use arguing with her about it though. And, it wasn't fair to yell at her. It was, after all, MY problem, and not hers. She didn't make the rules. It was information I should have collected while planning my hike.

I retreated to the hiker table and contemplated starting a revolution. I wanted to rally the hikers together and put up picket

61

signs, and chant things like "let the magic happen", and "trail angel lives matter". Instead I gorged myself on more cream filled cookies and decided I would try to Facetime with Charlie. I hadn't talked to him since we parted ways at Crater Lake. Unfortunately, I wouldn't have this option to contact my son since he was without an IPhone, and staying with his biological dad.

Although the Wi-Fi connection was spotty and delayed, at best, it was nice to see his smiling face. We chatted about how to get my gear home, and he told me he'd make some calls.
"Where is Kona?" I asked
"She has been in the den," he said.

When I am home, Kona stays by my side at all times. When I leave for work or head out for the day she retreats to the den and lays under the desk.

I watched Charlie walk through the house, from the screen of my phone, as he called out for Kona. I finally saw her, she was laying under the desk and wagged her tail.
"She hasn't been sleeping in the bedroom much," he said.
"She lays in here a lot."
Kona always sleeps in her bed, on my side of the bed, when I am home.

Charlie pointed his phone at Kona so I could see her, and with any luck she would see my face on the phone screen.
"Kona!" I called out to her.

Kona stood and looked up all around the room.
"Where is mom?" Charlie asked her, and then Kona went to the back door, anxiously looking outside, confused.
"That was a bad idea!" I managed to choke out. Seeing how confused she was instantly put me into tears.

Not too long after hanging up, Charlie messaged to tell me that our Sargent from Search and Rescue made a call to a buddy from the local sheriffs unit.

"A deputy will come to Shelter Cove and pick up the package."

I was thrilled! Thank you Charlie and Thank you Sarg! I was expecting the deputy to be there within the next thirty minutes or so. A couple hours drug by, and soon I was becoming fearful that he wasn't going to be able to make it.
"He must have got a call." I messaged Charlie.

More weekend campers flooded past the hiker table, stopping every so often to ask questions.

"I took my first shower in five days today," I told one couple. "All you can really hope for out here is clean teeth and clean fingernails. Everything else is pointless to try to keep up!" I joked. Mike and Brooke were staying in a cabin in the cove. They were visiting from California.

"What's your trail name" asked Mike.

"Two-Sips" I said confidently.

"What happens after three sips?" he questioned, laughing.

"We didn't find out!" I laughed back.

Hours had passed, and before I knew it, the UPS truck pulled into the cove. It was 6PM. Still no deputy. I waited for the UPS driver to unload the packages from the truck, and I followed eagerly behind him as he took the boxes into the store. The clerk was standing there as I and a few other hikers crowded around.

"Let me get these checked in and then you can sign for your package," she told us with one hand up, as if to fend us off.

She received my package, and then had me sign her clip board. I scooped up the small box and headed back to the table with it. I pulled out my knife and slowly cut through the packaging tape. The grey and bright orange nylon fabric was wrapped in thick bubble tape. I practically ran back to the camp site to tear down my tarp, and get my new tent up. After carefully reading through the instructions, I had the tent set up in just a few minutes. It was so easy! I stood there for a few minutes staring in awe.

I messaged Charlie, "Love the tent!" and I sent him a picture of it. It was getting dark and I needed to get my chargers from the hiker area. On the way back I ran into Mike and Brooke.

"Is everything OK", they asked.

"I'm worried... I have all this gear to send back home, and..." I told them the whole story about "no trail angels allowed", and the deputy not being able to get away to pick up package.

"We can send it out for you", they offered.

"REALLY?" I said excitedly.

"I can leave you money... I need to get cash. The store opens around 7AM...I'll use the ATM, and then I can leave the box with all my information."

Mike and Brooke agreed and gave me their cabin number.

"Well, don't tell any of the workers here," I leaned in as if telling a secret, "but you're officially trail angels", I said to them and winked.

63

I was feeling so grateful, and I messaged Charlie one last time for the night to tell him the good news. After sending the message, I tucked myself into my tent, and listened to the wind blow gently against the sides. I felt so much safer and cozy in my tent. I fell asleep fast, and slept hard through the night.

Day fifteen

I woke around 5AM to the usual sounds of thru-hikers packing up their camps. The sounds of air mattresses deflating, zippers zipping and unzipping, and lightweight materials being squeezed into stuff sacks. I followed suit and carefully packed my tent; rolling it tightly and attaching it to the outside of my pack.

It was heavier than my tarp and bivy combo, but I was convinced already it would be worth the few extra ounces. I had two things on my mind to accomplish before heading back on the trail: get cash from the ATM, and order an espresso. I arrived at the hiker table at 6:00AM. I would have to kill sixty minutes before the store opened. I made my way to the bathroom, and also made sure to feel some genuine gratitude for the flushing toilet.

I wasn't sure how long it would be before I would come across another one of those! I reorganized some things in my pack, and made some oatmeal. At 7AM I climbed the steps to the store and pulled on the door handle. It was locked. I peered into the windows, and the lights were off.

"They opened at 7AM yesterday!" I thought to myself. I glanced down to notice an hours of operation sign. The store wouldn't open until 8AM today. I needed to leave. I pulled out my plastic baggie wallet, and I counted out a few dollars in cash, and some quarters. It was all of the cash I had left. I put the money in an envelope with a thank you note addressed to Mike and Brooke.

"I hope it is enough," I thought, and I quietly placed my box of gear on the porch of their cabin.

"Thank you so much", I whispered to Mike and Brooke, who were probably sound asleep in the cabin, as I tip-toed away.

After leaving Shelter Cove, and crossing over the railroad tracks, I found my way to the PCT intersection and began a gradual climb up the trail. It felt good to be hiking again. I felt stronger physically, and mentally. My spirits were renewed with the addition of my new tent. Even better, the rumor was that clear and sunny skies were in store for the next few days. I stopped on a bluff and looked out over Odelle Lake. Shelter Cove looked so small, so far away. I stared across the lake and into the hills beyond the water. "I did that", I whispered to myself.

I had seventy-five miles or so to go before I would reach my next resupply and meet up with my husband's good friend Tianna, in Sisters. I looked over my maps again when I got to the Rosary Lakes. Water wasn't going to be too much of an issue through this stretch. I was sitting around PCT mile 1908, and the next documented water source was at mile 1915.

However, I liked to camp near a water source, and the next water source with a campsite was at Charlton lake; mile 1923. I had already hiked Six miles. This meant I would have about fifteen more miles to go. I ate a Snickers and contemplated the mileage. I felt good. I felt rested. I felt determined to start pushing out twenty mile days. "Just pretend like you haven't hiked at all today!" I gave myself a pep talk, "You can totally do fifteen miles, NO problem! So what if it is really twenty one?"

My pack was quite a bit heavier since it carried a fresh resupply, three liters of water, and the added tent weight.
"Ya, you're right, we totally got this!"

Before leaving the Rosary Lake area I sent a group message out to family, "At Rosary Lakes, google it, it is beautiful!"

Somehow I felt as though if everyone would look up the lake while I was standing right there I could feel closer to them.

The trail made its way up, climbing a little less than twelve-hundred feet or so over the next six miles, and then back down. I was stopping less to catch my breath, and powering through when I felt like I wanted to stop. I wasn't moving fast, but I was going steady. At 2:00pm I arrived at the "Eugene to PCT" trail junction. I messaged Charlie.
"Wish I had phone signal so we could talk more. If I take this side trail I think you can meet me in Eugene lol!"

I sat down and opened up a tuna pouch for lunch. Charlie messaged me back.
"Lol wish so to bb. Lol stay on course. Lol!"

For the first time I could joke about wanting to go home, and not be dying inside for him to come get me. I did miss him terribly, but this time I wasn't sobbing in the pouring rain, hiding under a table, or contemplating quitting. I was going to make my first twenty mile day, and I was determined to like it!

I was down to two liters of water, and bypassed the Bobby Lake trail junction. I began passing small ponds and lakes near the trail every one to three miles. Water was more abundant in this stretch than I had realized while studying the maps. I let myself get down to a half liter, and then refilled. But, I only refilled two liters. The forest cover was thick, and although sunny, the temperature was still cool enough that I wasn't drinking water in excess. I took the chance, and enjoyed the lighter pack weight!

It was funny to me that I had no idea what the actual temperature was, and I was starting to use my phone less to tell time. Back home I was accustomed to checking the weather reports daily. I had an alarm clock to rouse me from sleep, and a phone tethered to the palm of my hand during the day. All that I thought I needed was always just a few scrolls and a tap away.

On the trail, I was beginning to become in sync with the world around me and was learning to use all of my senses. The sun was my watch, the air and my skin were my thermostat, the birds were my alarm clock, and the shade of the trees was both my air conditioning and day time storm cover. Life was becoming simpler.

I ate only when I was hungry, and not because I was on a schedule that forced me to "eat now or you won't get to eat for three more hours."

I hadn't worn make up in two weeks, and I was beginning to like the way I looked without it. "So that's what you really look like?" I would joke after taking a picture of myself.

"Not too bad. You could use some tweezers, but all in all you're not going to scare anyone!" I hoped.

It made me wonder why I had been fussing with make-up for all these years. Why do any of us? I rarely ever left the house without make-up. Truthfully, I didn't believe anyone would want to see the real me. Hell, I wasn't used to seeing the real me! And the trail has a way of bringing out the real in all who dare to let it envelop them.

I had worn make-up since I was twelve years old, and the thought of being seen in public without it was terrifying. I had packed a small tube of foundation and a travel size mascara into my resupply box that was going to be shipped to Sisters Oregon. Why? Because I planned on going into public. Such chains we woman hold ourselves in.

Charlie messaged me around 5PM "Go bb goooo! You got it!!! Few more miles!"

Just before 6PM I arrived at Charlton Lake. I smiled from ear to ear. "You fucking did it!" I cheered to myself.

I did it, I had pushed out my first twenty mile day. Not only was it my first twenty, it was my first time going over twenty... twenty one miles! My tracker started to beep, incoming message, it was Charlie.

"You fucking rock baby!!!!! Throw out your tent, get some food and feel good! You did GREAT today bb!"

And I did just that. I chose the largest campsite I could find! Much too large for just myself, and I set up my tent.

I was still amazed at how easy it was to set up! I gathered some fire wood, and built a small fire in the large fire pit. I sent another message to Charlie, "Also set up tent n built fire in thirty minutes. I'm great when its sunny lol!"

My first twenty one mile day was a milestone for me in many ways. It marked the start of a renewed sense of determination and power. I was surer of myself than I had been before. Maybe I was really going to make it across Oregon! My tracker beeped with another incoming message. This time it was my mom.

"Holy cow. Great day. Get some well-deserved rest. Much love."

5. RELEASE

Day sixteen

I would wake often in the middle of the night, and listen to the sounds around me as I drifted back to sleep. Back home it was hard to get out of bed. I would constantly fight with the snooze button. On the trail my body jerked to a waking state before the sun rose, just as the birds began their song; eager to meet the day. But I didn't start moving right away. I laid there, often breathing in my gratitude, filling my empty places with the realization of what I was actually doing. Awake, and thankful it was no longer a dream.

Bear and Beaver were still asleep. They were a young couple, New Hampshire transplants that now lived in Portland Oregon, and had started at Crater Lake. I had invited them to join me around my campfire that evening. I had watched them as I sat near the fire, enviously, working together as one to set up camp and prepare their meals.

Bear helped me to gather more firewood while Beaver tucked their gear away and made camp. I missed Charlie. I missed the way he would set up the tarp for us. I was no tarp master, but Charlie, Charlie was the tarp origami champion. I am sure that if I said "Charlie, I want our shelter to look like a swan tonight", he could have done it for me...

I was happy to have Bear and Beaver's company, but after an hour or so of watching the two of them work together and some conversation between the three of us, I retreated to my tent. I wondered what Charlie and I would talk about if we were still hiking together. If we were camped together at Charlton Lake. But, I didn't feel like talking any more that night, so maybe it didn't really matter..

I rose from my tent and stretched my arms to the sky, on my tippy toes. My legs and hips were stiff.
"Yeah...go twenty-one miles she said...you got this she said...it will be fun she said..."
I bent forward and touched the earth at my feet. I stood straight and I pulled my forehead to the sky, and a burning pain shot down my neck. "Holy hell fire!" It felt like I had been jabbed in the side of the neck with a hot iron.

I grabbed the base of my neck and rubbed vigorously. Digging through my first aid kit, I pulled out the ibuprofen and swallowed downed four of them. I went to the edge of the lake to refill my water container, and noticed black and grey smoke billowing over the mountain across the lake.

I messaged Charlie, "is there a fire near me?"
He responded, "Not finding any. Only one I see is East of Bend".
I quickly got out my maps, found my location and the location of the smoke, and decided that if there was a new fire, it wasn't near my direction of travel, for now. But, knowing fire, I didn't want to stay too long. I gathered my things and left.

The trail wound through thick tree cover, past boulder piles, and between burnouts. I was moving slow. Slower than normal. My body ached, it burned from my neck to the tips of my toes. I stopped often to adjust my laces and check on my blisters. The pinky toe on my left foot was fully covered with one large blister. It was no longer a toe; Just one fiery blister wrapped around the bones. The skin all around it was swollen with liquid, and opaque. The nail bed was bright red and tender to touch. I tugged on the toenail, and a searing pain shot across my skin. Surely, this little piggy would be the first to lose a toenail. I ate a quick Ibuprofen snack, and wrapped the toe in moleskin.

Hiking was like drifting in and out of consciousness. One minute I was completely aware of my surroundings, the next minute I was lost in a deep trance.

"You don't even need to drink booze. I mean, my god, you've gone days between drinks out here...and even when you can drink you only have a couple...You have had more stress out here and handled it just fine without drinking..."

The truth was, drinking at home was a weak attempt to numb the anxiety of any stressful situation, no matter the real severity of the issue. I drank when I was sad, mad, and happy. Emotions were stressful! Most mornings I woke feeling ashamed of the empty bottle of wine sitting on the kitchen counter.

I continued to scold myself over my drinking habit…and then every other issue in my life began to fill the empty spaces around my thoughts; over and over again.

"Cole and Charlie are going to figure it out...you don't need to play referee every damn day... and you really don't need to work two jobs...you would have less stress if you had just one job…and imagine all the time you could spend with your family if you had just one job..."

I had been working two jobs for almost two years. Another attempt to make things "less stressful", but only on the checkbook. And before that, I spent five years earning my Bachelor degree, while working full time during the day. A lack of family time had been weighing on my heart for many years. I was carrying guilt for all of the trips I never took Cole on when he was a young boy, mostly because I was busy trying to be an adult.

Funny thing is when you stop drinking and start thinking about all the reasons why you drink, well…unexpected things come to the surface, and for once I was in a position to logically acknowledge them and try to deal with them. For me, it was easier to do this while I was out of the environment that held all my normal day to day stressors. The hard part was not being able to turn things off with day to day distractions.

"Family...maybe if you were home more, then Charlie and Cole could learn to get along better...there you go playing referee again...that's not your job...you're a good wife...you're a good mother" And then I'd break down, sobbing. Was I really a good mother? A good wife? Did I really believe that, or was I just trying to sway myself?

"That's good...there you go... Cry it out... Because you sure as hell aren't going to drink it away out here..."

I wasn't sure at that point if I wanted a bottle of wine or not. I just wanted to cry. I needed to cry. And I let myself finally feel it all without attempting to numb it. Without pushing it away. I let myself finally be angry, to be guilty, to be broken, and I let out a guttural wail. Crumpled over at the waist, I dropped my trekking poles and hugged myself tightly; squeezing my eyes shut. Something deep inside me became unlocked.

My only true coping skills in life, up until this point, had been tuning things out or drinking things away. My mind was suddenly bombarded with emotions and memories. Things I hadn't thought of in years. Memories as a child, regrets as a young adult; disappointment and rage. I couldn't shut it off. All I could do was feel. I didn't know what to do with all of it, and so I cried, harder than I had ever cried in my entire life.

I sat little-bit (my back pack) down against the trail and laid my trekking poles at her side. I called them North Pole and South Pole. South Pole was always held in my left hand. It was just part of the routine now. I sat down in the shrubs along the trail and stared up at the sky. It was so blue it made me gasped. I wiped my tears and thought, "the only time I've seen blue like that is looking at Charlie's eyes", and it was true.

What I would have given to see him at that moment. Charlie and I had been a couple for almost ten years. We had taken a trip back east together the summer before. We attended Tom Brown Jr's survival school in the Pine Barrens of New Jersey. Tom told the class, "Know what you love…" I loved my husband. But I had never looked into his eyes the way I stared at the sky. And he certainly had never seen me in the emotional state I was in now. I never had really shared how much I kept buried away. He loved me, but there was so much I didn't let him see of me. How could he really know me?

I wished I was staring into his eyes. I wanted to look at him. To be grateful in his presence. To really see him, in a way that showed him how much I truly appreciate his being. Because I did. And I wasn't sure, in that moment, if he really knew how much I needed him. Surely I was too brazen and independent to let him know how much I depended on him.

Our first time hiking to Pilot Rock marked our longest day hike together, in 2012. We scrambled up the shale rock, stopping to catch our breath often over the steep slippery rock. Charlie made his way ahead of me, and stopped on a flat area. He continued on as I stopped and turned to look below me. The earth shifted under my feet, and I pictured myself sliding down the rock face.

I couldn't move...I was frozen with fear. I looked up to see Charlie waiting for me to make my next move, and I started to cry, uncontrollably. His lips were moving but all I could hear was the sound of my heartbeat and my breathing. He stretched out his hand towards me.

"You're OK," he said, "I got you!"

I took his hand.

"I can't move." I whimpered.

If I haven't said it yet I will say it now, I am terrified of heights!

Charlie began to walk me through my footing, "Put your right foot here...Now, take a step with your left foot...I got you...you can do it. Now grab on to the rock here. Keep coming forward..."

Charlie walked me through the next ten feet or so, until I was safe in his arms.

"DON'T tell ANYONE I cried!" I sobbed and half laughed.

We never did make it to the top of pilot rock.

"Let's just have lunch here" I suggested.

We sat together eating our lunch, watching the other day hikers make their way to the top and scramble back down the rock..

I hiked along, staring at the sky, pretending to gaze into Charlie's eyes. I was feeling low. Was it the miles I put in the day before? Maybe it was the emotional roller coaster I was riding. The sudden release of years of pent up emotions and thoughts.

I messaged Charlie around 2PM, "Stopping for another break. So tired today."

I was tired, physically. But the truth of the matter is I was tired mentally.

It was just that I didn't want him to know how mentally exhausted I was. I didn't want him to worry more about me. I didn't know how to express in a short text message how sorry I was that I had never truly appreciated how amazingly blue his eyes were, or about the one thousand other things that were creeping into my head. Charlie urged me to find a closer stopping point.

"Gonna go five more to horseshoe lake." I responded, and by 4:40PM I had covered eighteen miles total, "Made it!" I told him.

I made camp and began to tend to my blisters. Horseshoe Lake was more like a giant pond, but it was beautiful. I cooked up "Chicken Gumbo", and mixed Abualita's Mexican hot chocolate and Starbucks instant coffee. I drained my blisters and sat on a log next to an abandoned camp fire pit.

I suddenly felt strangely calm after my day of feeling low, after the explosion of emotions, and missing Charlie so much. I set up camp in record time. I was never one to get used to routines, but I had my camp routine down pat! I unpacked everything in order, and every piece of equipment suddenly had a place and a sequence of being unpacked.

I ate my dinner down like I was starving, and I sipped on my wilderness mocha like I was the queen of the forest. I watched dragon flies dance on the water, and the rays of the setting sun filled the spaces between the lower tree limbs around me.

I sent Charlie another message before heading to bed before 7PM, "Thank u for all the support bb".

And He replied, "It's my purpose love. Xoxo"...

6. LAVA

I lay there, very still. The smell of sweat mixed with trail dust filled the compact space of my one person tent. As the sun sank behind the trees I heard footsteps. My ears perked up, and I listened closer.

Stomp...stomp...stomp....stomp... Then the sound of brush being pushed aside. Whatever it was, I could tell that it had four feet, and it was walking heavy.

I waited, staring out of my unzipped rain fly. It sounded like it was getting closer. I took my gun from under my sleeping bag, and sat up as quietly as I could. I started to unzip my tent slowly, as to not startle whatever was prowling around just feet from my campsite. I held the gun in my right hand, and poked my head slowly outside of my tent, looking to the far left, where I knew it stood.

Thankfully, there stood Beaver and Bear!
"Hey!" said Beaver, "I hope we didn't wake you!"
I laughed out loud, and concealed my weapon swiftly.
"Not at all!" I almost shouted trying to hide my relief.
"There is more room over here!" I invited them again to my campsite.

They declined the invite and began to set up camp just down the trail, but still in sight.
"You made great mileage today!" I cheered to them.

Bear and Beaver had been hiking ten to twelve miles per day since they had left Crater Lake. Today they covered eighteen miles. I sunk back into my tent and sleeping bag.

"Way to go Two-sips!" I reprimanded myself.

"Way to almost shoot up the place!"

"Hey, shut up, at least I was right about the whole four legged thing!" I snapped back to myself smugly.

Day seventeen

In the morning I rose and left camp before Bear and Beaver showed any sign of life, again. The trail remained in its place, right where I left it, and I hopped back on it as if that was exactly what I was meant to do. I had no idea how far I had actually gone in total. I could estimate the miles, but I never really did the math. I thought it might be better if I treated every day like a day hike. Maybe I wouldn't feel as tired; maybe I wouldn't feel like I had been gone for so long, or maybe I just didn't want to know when the end of my hike was drawing near.

The tree cover was thick, and I began to grow weary of not having a view. Every now and again I would get a glimpse of one of the Sisters mountains in the distance. It kept me going. I knew the closer I got to the Three Sisters, the closer I was to meeting up with Tianna and spending a couple days with her and her family, eating real food, sleeping in a real bed, and taking a real shower.

At 10:20AM I stopped for a snack and refilled my water from an ice cold spring. Some thru-hikers whizzed by. Stopping only for a moment to find out how far I was hiking and how far I had already come. I pulled out my battery pack and electronic cigarette. The battery pack was down to two bars. This meant I could probably charge everything I had once more, or twice, before having to save the rest to keep my tracker charged. I had promised Charlie that my number one charging priority would be my satellite tracker. After a fifteen minute break I put everything back in little-bit's top pouch, and carried on.

As I hiked I fixed my eyes at the ground, scanning the trail ahead of me. I remembered what our friend Duran said, "Enjoy every moment, even the mundane." Things were definitely feeling mundane on this day!

"You will miss this too Crystal", I told myself.

"Left...right. Left...repeat..." I repeated our friend Eric's words of long distance hiking wisdom.

Suddenly, I crested a saddle.

Ahead of me was South Sister, and below me a valley that dipped into Elk Lake. I was tempted to take the two mile detour down to the lodge and take a half day gorging myself on burgers and homemade huckleberry ice cream, but I decided against self-induced lactose intolerant pain.

After taking a few photos, and deciding Charlie and I would most definitely return to Elk Lake resort soon, I noticed that my phone battery was at 50%. I reached into the top pouch of my pack and dug out the baggie that held my recharging gear.

"Funny...where is my phone cord?"

I sat down in the dirt and emptied the pouch completely, sifting through each item, one by one. No phone cord.

"SHIT!"

I opened the main compartment, and dug out a few items. No hiding phone cord.

"Way to go! I bet you left it at that creek over four miles away!" I sneered at myself.

"Just slow down and stop panicking". I repacked everything in its place, and decided to go a little farther, find a better spot to sit and recheck my gear. The phone cord had to be in the pack somewhere.

I made the steady climb up Koosah Mountain around 2:00PM, and began searching through my gear once I had made it to the top. Nothing... The charging cord to my phone was nowhere to be found. I sat, thinking of what lay before me, before I would reach my resupply in Sisters. My heart sank, Obsidian falls!

I thought that maybe, I could spread dad's ashes there. I also thought about how much Cole would love to see the pictures of the limited entry area. He loves Obsidian. My phone was my only camera, and it would die tonight, no doubt, without a way to charge it.

"You're a god damn genius"... Said half of me with a hateful tone. The other half of me chimed in... "What are you so worried about? Sayin' don't worry... bout a thing....Everything has worked out so far...right?"

And without thinking too much more about it, I began to pray. "Thank you so very much for taking care of me this far... I appreciate your strength, and the immense determination that you instill within me each day..." I continued, "Thank you for this beautiful trail, the wilderness, and the ability to see it with my whole heart... I am so grateful... I have a feeling that maybe the charging cord is in my sleeping bag. But, I am going to trust that you will help me when I need it. So I am not going to dig it out now. I am going to have faith that you are taking care of the things I can't... And I know I just need to allow faith to be part of my journey and what I am learning out here, Amen."

By 3:40 I was starting to feel the worry creeping back into my gut and I messaged Charlie, "Can't find phone cord!!! Might have fallen out at one of my stops, miles ago."

By 4:40 I messaged Charlie again, "20% on phone. Really wanted pics of obsidian falls tomorrow."

By 5:00 I had been hiking through some of the prettiest area that I had ever seen in my life. I was too afraid to take many pictures. Afraid my phone would die and then I would have nothing to take pictures with tomorrow if I decided to spread my dad's ashes. I was mentally exhausted from the stress of it all by 5:45, when I reached the North Fork Mesa Creek.

The water was hardly running at the creek, and I decided to go down farther. I followed the trail a for couple more miles before hitting the mother-load of glacier run off. I found a decent camp site, and began unpacking my gear. I had taken a leap of faith that I would find more water and a better camp site than the first creek, surely my charging cord would magically appear; just as the abundant water had.

"I know it's in here!" I said out loud, as if I needed to convince God to take it out of hiding; as if I was not doubting he had heard me.

I pulled out the stuff sack that compressed my sleeping bag, and tore the bag out of it. I shook it upside down, never doubting that the cord would come tumbling out. Nothing! I shook it again. I turned it inside out. Still nothing!

"But, How?" I wondered. "
This is the last place I charged my phone!"
I was in my sleeping bag, and I had it plugged in. It has to be here!"
I shook the bag vigorously, and started to become angry, "I had faith damn it!" I yelled in my head to God.

"REAL unwavering faith that it was going to be here! SO WHAT if it was over a phone cord... I haven't had that kind of faith in years... Grrrr!"

I became angrier, and I turned back to my pack, on an impulsive mission to start dumping the rest of its contents. There,

lying next to my pack in the dirt, under the stuff sack that had held my sleeping bag, was the white USB charging cord. I literally started to laugh out loud through a burst of tears.
"Well played God! Well played!" I shook my head.
"Thank you for not quitting on me. I whispered sheepishly.
And I wondered, who was testing who?

The dense forest quickly grew dark once the sun fell below the tree line. I used my head lamp to look over my maps, and plan my mileage for the next day.

A month or so before the hike, Charlie had figured out how to download Halfmile's way points into google earth. We would sit together with the laptop and "fly" the trail, I was fascinated and eager to see the trail in real life. The trail was marked by a deep red line on the satellite image on the computer screen. We scanned over the lava field area; a maroon and open area with barely any trees.
"See, It will be really hard to get lost.. I mean look," I pointed to the screen, "the trail is bright red!" I said sarcastically.
Charlie laughed and shook his head at me. He looks at me like that a lot. I went to the desk top and pulled up pictures of the lava fields and the limited entry Obsidian Falls area. I was particularly excited about the lava fields. I had never seen anything like it before in my life. "I'm gonna be there! I'm gonna know what it feels like to be there." I gazed at the screen, awestruck.

Day eighteen

After repacking most of my gear the next morning, I sipped on coffee and reviewed my route for the day, again. It was twenty miles from my campsite to the Lava Lake Campground. Once to the campground, Tianna would pick me up and take me to her home in Sisters for a couple nights. I compared mental notes to how long it had taken me to hike eighteen to twenty-one miles each day, and figured I would reach the campground by 6PM. I refilled my water and turned on my tracker at 7:43, "Starting day."
The trail wound its way through the thick forest, fallen trees, and dense forest shrubs. After a few miles South Sister towered over me and the tree line. I stood, gazing at her. I walked slowly, taking in

the new views around me. Soon the land around me opened up into large meadows and a valley. I stopped near a sparkling pond and took the opportunity to sit in silence for a few moments.

I felt overwhelmed with gratitude.

Charlie messaged me on my tracker, "WOW!!! Bet the view is awesome bb!"

I replied, "Yeah. Had to stop a minute. We need to come back here!"

I took comfort in knowing that Charlie and my mom were watching my every move, for the most part. I was out there alone, but there were eyes in the sky that could see the terrain, and what I was seeing (kind of). And they could see me moving along the trail. Even though "me" was a little blue dot moving as the crow flies on a satellite image of the area. Even still, made me feel like I was able to share a part of my journey with them in real time.

My stomach growled as I hiked along. I had eaten breakfast, but I felt famished. The waist belt on my pack kept creeping up my lower back, and I couldn't get it cinched down tight enough around the tops of my shrinking hips.

"Bacon! I want bacon, on a burger, with extra cheese, extra mayo, lots of onions!" I daydreamed as I hiked.

"I want a salad, with hard boiled eggs, more bacon... Oh, and lots of blue cheese dressing!"

My mouth watered. I rounded a corner, and saw a shaded area under a large tree. It was the perfect sitting spot, and I half expected Slip N Slide to sitting there.

"He would like it here!" I smiled to myself, and wondered about what he was doing now in Germany.

The tree trunk made a large L formation, and called for someone to rest in her shade. I sat my pack at the tree's side, and clambered on to the trunk, stretching out, and not paying too much attention to the sap that I was sitting in.

I messaged Charlie, "Stopped to eat. Daydreaming of bacon cheese burgers!"

I reached the limited entry area just before 1PM. I was a little behind schedule, distracted by all the beauty around me.

"Maybe this is where I will leave you dad!" I thought.

Maybe today was the day I spread my dad's ashes. But I knew I had to find the perfect spot.

Small flecks of black obsidian littered the trail and forest floor. Large black and shiny boulders protruded from the hills around me. Soon, I could hear the sound of the creek and the falls in the distance.

My excitement grew as the roar of the waters got louder. I thought about all of the images I had seen on the computer back home, and thought "here it comes, you're going to see it in real life and you walked all the way here to do it!"

I stood at the base of the waterfall in awe. It wasn't as tall as I had expected, but it was beautiful. The fresh clean water rushed over the hill above me, and cut through the mountain side, creating a rushing stream that flowed out of sight below. Black obsidian was scattered in the creek bed; crushed and eroded from the waters magnificent power.

I watched day hikers make their way down to the falls from the trail above from the day hike entry route, and decided, that even though amazing, this wasn't going to be the place I spread dads ashes. It was good. A pretty spot, but not good enough to honor the end of his journey. I made the short but steep climb back to the trail, and stopped to look over my map. The lava fields were next. Opie Dilldock Pass was about 2.5 miles away. Maybe that is where I would leave dad.

"It's a pretty tough climb," said Chris, back at Shelter Cove. "but it is really beautiful up there!"
"OPIE DILLDOCK? That climb sucks!" James chimed in, laughing. "But, yeah, it would be a nice place to spread your dad's ashes," he said with a hint of sarcasm.

I looked at the contour lines of my map. It was going to be quite the climb! It was almost 2PM, and I had only gone about ten miles so far. The trail quickly turned from obsidian meadows to barren layers of cinder. I marched uphill. It felt like every step I would take forward I would slide a half a step back on the lava rock.

The rocks were the size of small apples and large plums, and under them a layer of smaller lava rocks mixed with scree. The sun beat down on me, and by 3:00PM I was making my way up Opie Dilldock pass.

This climb was no joke. The trail wound up multiple switchbacks, about forty feet long, and up the hill about twenty feet (only my best guess). I stopped dreaming of bacon and started wishing for teleportation powers.

I had reached a false summit of sorts when two teenage boys appeared, bouncing down the lava rock; all smiles with their day packs.

"Hey!", one of the boys said to me, "When you get to the top, take the side trail on the right to check out the view...totally worth the extra quarter mile!"

"Yeah? Fuck off!" is what I wanted to say, but I smiled and asked, "So I'm almost to the top?"

"Yeah, almost there, gotta check it out!" And they trotted past me down the switch backs.

At the top I took off my pack and guzzled down some water. A lot of water. I looked around and decided against trying to find the view point the boys had suggested to me. I also looked around and thought of spreading my dad's ashes.

"No... This place reminds me of hell. Not really the kind of place you want to leave your loved one!"

I stared out into the distance. It was an amazing view. The lava fields stretched out for miles. Ridge lines and peaks danced on the horizon. There was hardly a cloud in sight, and the only sound was that of the wind. But as I hiked on I wanted nothing more than to be done with the lava fields.

The trail led me up, and soon I was winding around lava cliffs.

"It is a good thing my mom can't REALLY see me." I joked.

I could hear her scolding me as a child, "Crystal Lee! Get your butt down from there!"

I stood on a high point, the sun beating down on me and my water getting low, when my tracker started to beep; incoming message.

It was my mom, "Hope you are having a good day. Love you so much. You are such a strong amazing girl!"

I desperately wanted to message her and say, "Mommy, will you come get me?"

But instead I replied, "Right now I hate lava rock lol!"

Without skipping a beat, mom reached out and as great moms do, and gave me just enough to keep moving, "Yes. I can see on tracker that is what u r dealing with. Be careful..." She wrote.

It was especially touching at the moment, knowing my mom was so afraid for me to be going on this journey alone. I stood there quietly for a moment, remembering many of the times my mom had been there for me. This moment was no different. I took a deep breath.

The hot air burned my nostrils, and then a cool breeze brushed against my ears and cheeks.

"Gotta keep moving," I urged myself.

Soon the lava field turned back into a meadow, and Minnie Scott Spring crossed the trail. I debated taking off all of my gear and laying in the shallow ice cold water. Instead I sat next to it, and dug down into the water's bed to make a spot deep enough to fill my water bottle. I drank down one liter, and began to refill again when someone yelled out, "Hello!"

I looked up and a thru-hiker stood about one hundred feet away, waving at me. We introduced ourselves as I kept refilling.

"My name's Data." he said.

"Two-Sips." I replied.

We exchanged the regular "I'm thru-hiking, and I'm Section hiking" intros, and then he was off. He was fast! Hell, he must have been running up Opie Dilldock, because I never saw him coming while I was there. I was moving so slow.

It was just after 5PM when I messaged Tianna to tell her I still had five more miles to go.

"Probably closer to 7:30", I told her.

I glanced over my map, 7:30 was a long shot at my current pace and I really didn't want to be out here much longer! The five miles ahead of me were mostly more lava fields. I thought about it, ate an extra Snickers: I decided that I was going to have to run some of it!

The sun beat down on me as my feet picked up the pace.

"You've got this! You told her you'd be there at 7:30PM! You can do it! You can make it!"

The trail turned down hill and I began to run. My pack, loose around my shrinking waist, rocked violently against my tail bone. I could hear the clanging of my stove and other gear rattling inside as I ran down hill. I was desperate to make it to Lava Lake campground to meet Tianna; maybe not on time but as soon as possible.

The lava rock slipped and rolled under foot.

"The last thing you need is to roll an ankle"! I scolded myself.

I rounded a corner and at the bottom of the hill I saw three people. It was Data, and two others that looked to be two day hikers. After coming to a screeching halt and walking towards them trying to be nonchalant, I reached the small "crowd" after a few seconds.

"Wow! You caught up to me fast!" Data exclaimed.

I stopped to chat out of politeness. "Yeah," I said gulping down my breathlessness, "got to really take advantage of all the downhill you know!"

I SO sounded like SUCH a section hiker...desperate for a bacon cheese burger.

I left the three of them on the trail in my wake of despair. The day hikers were very interested in hearing about Data's thru-hike. I doubted that anyone, at the moment, wanted to hear about my solo Oregon journey.

I was OK with not talking about myself. I was more concerned that the sun would be setting soon and that I had real food to eat in town. Even better, I would be DONE with the lava fields.

"Jesus? How late do stores stay open in Sisters?" I was suddenly worried that the small town would be closed down by the time I got there. "Do they have fast food"?

"Please God let me be done with the lava fields." I begged silently between food prayers.

After a mile or so of jogging with my forty something pound pack, over hills and past more lava fields, the landscape around the trail turned into a more wooded area, uphill, and then back to lava field. I could smell fresh water. I couldn't see it, but I could smell it. This was a new gift that had been brought to my attention near the beginning of Three Sisters Wilderness.

It was something amazing to know that, by scent, I was near fresh water. It wasn't long before I reached Mathieu Lake Trail. Just three more miles to go. I kept up the pace, and every downhill I took the opportunity to run as fast as I could. I tried to ignore how badly I was hurting, and the fact that I wanted to be done for the day. I could enjoy myself more if I wasn't so focused on how DONE I felt. I forced myself to stop occasionally and take in the view around me; not moving on until I regained some gratitude. Another trail gift, the gift of time to stop and appreciate the world around you.

Soon I was on flat ground made of dirt. Actual, dusty, brown, powdery DIRT! I ran! I ran fast! The dust of the trail spun up around my feet and tickled my nostrils. I held both north and south poles in my right hand, and I ran like I was five years old: chasing a unicorn.

About a half mile from Lava Lake campground trail junction I ran past an older woman, and she grinned at me. A few seconds later I passed a young lady (Who I assumed was her twenty something year old daughter) and the young girl stopped in her tracks. Our eyes met as I ran past, and she said in slow motion.. "Wow!" Her gaze set on me.

All I could think of were my friends back home, who ran for fun. I had tried running for fun a few times. But I never could seem to believe there was actually any FUN involved, as much as I wanted to love it; until this day! "I am so going to run a couple of 5k's with them!"

But today I wasn't running for fun. I was running for bacon. And because I wanted to be done. And because I had told Tianna I would meet her at a certain time. And I had no time left to spare. My leg muscles twitched and burned with each pounding stride. My backpack bounced against me, and sweat rolled down my forehead. I was almost there!

The trail junction for Lava Lake campground cut off to the right, and I walked the last quarter mile into the sea of cars parked in the parking lot. My OR/WA guide book had said this was a good place for a hitch into sisters. The parking lot was full of cars, and I could hear people talking, dogs barking, and kids squabbling in the distance.

I Messaged Tianna at 7:42pm "I'm in parking area."

I sat down in the dusty red dirt, with no care. I took a deep breath and stared at the light blue sky; the sun was getting low, almost out of sight. My feet throbbed and the muscles twitched in my thighs. I didn't make my 7:30 deadline, exactly, but I had cut it close. I messaged Charlie ten minutes later, "I'm so done for day lol." He responded almost instantly, "WAY TO GOOOOO BABY!"

I had started to complain that I was a couple hours later than I had anticipated at the start of that morning. But then I realized, I was a day ahead of schedule of my original hiking plan.

Within an hour, Tianna and her husband pulled into the dusty turn around to pick me up. I was tired. It was close to 9PM, and way past my bedtime. I felt like I had been drug from battle and was ready to surrender. I clambered into the vehicle and we headed down the highway. I steadied my gaze on the white line of the highway.

I hadn't moved faster than a few miles an hour in a long time. I centered my vision in an attempt to not to be car sick, and asked if we could still go to the grocery store, and tried to disguise my anxious tone. It was late and I didn't want to feel like a burden, but I had never been so hungry and so tired at the same time.

"Of course!" Tianna said, and they graciously drove me to the grocery store.

During the drive, the scent of my own body filled the air around me. It had been days since my last real shower, and I prayed that I wasn't too offensive to my kind friends. Inside the store I grabbed a grocery cart, and made my way towards the Deli. I was sure that is where all the greasiest food would be!

I was saddened to find that all the hot food had been cleared for the day, but then a lone container of hot deli macaroni and cheese caught my eye. My mouth watered as I put it in the cart. I pushed the cart forward, into the produce section and snatched up a large Cobb salad, then a quart of organic mango lemonade. I headed for the snack aisles and snatched up a package of cream filled cookies, and a box of Cheeze-it Grooves. Then I made a detour for the beer cooler and I chose a chocolate stout.

Walking towards the checkout stand, a group of three teenage boys passed me. Two of them about broke their necks, staring back at me. One of them laughed and whispered something to the other. The other chuckled. The three of them then all looked back at me over their shoulders. I smiled, and then realized how out of place I looked.

I had left my back pack in the car. I wished I had it on. Maybe they would realize I was a hiker and not just a smelly person. I wanted to blurt out "I normally don't smell this bad!"

But why did I care...? It was now my turn in the checkout line and I pulled a small plastic baggy out of my back pocket. It contained my driver's license, my debit card, and receipts from Shelter Cove. The cashier smiled, but I could tell by the look in her eyes she was just being polite, and probably holding her breath.
"Have a nice night," she said, and as I grabbed up my grocery bag I winked at her.
"Oh, I plan on it!" I smiled and walked out the double doors.

We pulled into the driveway. I turned on my phone, hoping to get cell signal to call Charlie, but no luck. Tianna showed me to the bedroom that I would be staying in, and I put my pack on the floor. Her girls were gone, visiting their grandma. I thought maybe I should shower before I ate, but then I thought "what is one more baby wipe bath gonna hurt?"

I wiped down, and put on my "clean" town clothes.

I curled up on the couch with my beer and deli mac n cheese.

After the mac and cheese I began to devour the box of salty snack crackers. The three of us chatted in the living room for some time about hunting, tracking, hiking, and being outdoors. Maybe it was the lava fields, or maybe it was the beer. Maybe it was days of hiking. But I couldn't keep my eyes open any longer. I retreated to the bedroom.

The room was decorated just as any little girl would dream. Horses, unicorns, paisley, stuffed animals, and piggy banks. I unloaded my gun, and placed it on the small white dresser beside the bed. I plugged in my phone charger, and climbed on to the bottom bunk bed. I tucked in and felt the cool summer breeze flow in from the window. Their cat, "Charlie", snuggled up next to me and pawed at my chest.

I missed my own Charlie. And I missed my son. I tried messaging them again, but no cell service. It was almost midnight and there was not one nerve in my body that could fight to stay awake any longer. I laid there, and drifted off to the sound of the cat purring against my cheek.

Day nineteen

I awoke. The room was dark, and silent. No birds. I drifted back to sleep. I woke again and the cool morning air filled the room. I lay there, waiting for the sun. Waiting for the sound of the birds. My alarm sounded from my phone on the night stand and Bob Marley sang "Three little birds"... I snatched up my phone, and Charlie the cat scampered off of the bed, meowing at the door.

I stretched my legs. They stiffened half way through the stretch. I took a deep breath. I got up and the cold hardwood floors stung my feet and strained my arches. It was strange to feel flooring under foot after so many mornings in the dirt. I gathered up my toiletries, and peeked out into the hall way. The light was on in Tianna's bedroom, but I didn't see anyone; so I made a beeline for the bathroom, just a few feet from the bedroom door.

Closing the door behind me, I admired the shower surrounded in clean glass and tile. "I hope I don't make a mess of this!" I thought.

I turned on the water and waited for the steam to rise. Stepping into the hot waterfall of clear water felt heavenly. I washed, shaved, scrubbed. My hair was falling out even more. I made a point to gather up as much of my locks from the drain as I could catch.

"YOU need a cheese burger!" I reprimanded myself.

After showering and dressing, I smeared a small amount of foundation on my face, and a thin layer of mascara. Tianna and I made our way to REI. I decided long ago, on the trail, that I would need some insoles, and some sort of jacket; as I had opted to leave my down jacket behind at home.

At the REI in Bend, I tried on some Super Feet insoles, and found a Columbia fleece jacket. I also picked up some extra Gu-gels and other caffeinated snacks. We then made our way to Worthy Brewing Company. Everything on the menu sounded enticing, but I was scanning the menu for bacon. I finally decided on a burger with bacon (of course), sweet potato fries, and ordered an Atlas blackberry cider to go with it. My mouth watered in anticipation. Tianna insisted on buying my meal.

"You earned it!" She said to me kindly.

We sat and chatted like we had known each other for years, only, this was the first time she and I had really sat down alone together. I was happy to be with someone who I shared so much past with, but who I didn't really know. It felt like sitting with old friends, and old friends are hard to come by. When you find them, you should keep them. Even if the only past you share is with someone close to you. In this case, my husband.

After shopping and lunch was done, we headed to Jason's grandmother's house. Grandma, as I call her now, was preparing a meal for us. She made us elk steak stroganoff from scratch, and lemon-ginger vodka martinis with a sugar rim (from fresh squeezed lemons and Crater Lake Vodka). I had two, though I could have had five, and I reluctantly declined a third. But my inner voice was warning me, "Control yourself, you have got some walking to do tomorrow!"

We sat around the table together, passed the components of the meal, and shared our laughter. It felt like so long since I had shared in a true family experience. I didn't want to leave, but began to grow worried when I realized the sun would soon be setting, and I would soon be needing to hit the trail, and early.

After we returned to the house, I looked over my maps that I had sent myself in a resupply box. I became anxious when I saw MORE lava fields on the map. Not as much as I had previously walked through, but I had thought I was DONE with them! I was done with them, mentally, just not literally! I would have to endure a few more miles. Just the thought of it pained me.

Day twenty

I awoke to the smell of breakfast cooking. Tianna was up early, making huckleberry pancakes. I repacked my gear, as Tianna brought me my laundry that she had washed and folded for me the night before. On the way back to Lava Lake campground, we stopped at an espresso shop, and I ordered the last coffee I would see until Ollalie Lake, four days away.

The creamy white chocolate mocha made its way around the huckleberry pancakes and warmed my soul. I gulped down the last of it as we pulled into the parking area, knowing I couldn't take it with me on the trail. Tianna and I hugged goodbye, and I found my way back to the trail junction that would lead me back onto the PCT.

The PCT quickly turned from a powdery dirt trail, into a cinder trail once again. I pushed myself forward with my back foot, and my front foot slid backwards, rolling under the lava rock and scree. The sun beat down on me before 9AM, and it had only been an hour since I was dropped off.

"Jesus, where am I?" I complained. Mordor?"

Before the lava fields were completely done, the area around me turned into a complete burnout area. The trees around me were white and charred. After a long stretch of not seeing anyone on the trail since the Mackenzie pass parking area, some south bound hikers appeared.

"Will you take our picture", one of them asked.

I put north and south pole against a charred tree, and held the camera up.

"Did it take?" I asked them. I took one more just in case.

"Thanks!" They said as they practically ran off towards the town of Sisters.

"Ugh! You should have asked them about the river crossings! Dumb, Crystal!" I scolded myself.

I had a couple of so called dangerous river crossings coming up, and a south bounder would be the perfect type of hiker to ask about said river crossings.

A "south bounder", also called a SOBO for short, is a hiker headed South on the trail, usually from the Canadian border to the Mexican border. These gems are less common then NOBO's, and can offer some good insights on the trail ahead! Up until now, I had only met hikers traveling north.

After another mile or so, I saw someone else coming down the trail ahead of me. As he got closer I looked over his gear to deduce whether he was a SOBO PCT hiker or a section hiker. He had long dark hair, a smaller Osprey pack, and a smart-water water bottle with a Sawyer Squeeze water filter. He looked like he most definitely was one of the pack!

"Hey!" I called out to him as he approached.

"Hello," he replied.

"Did you start at the top?" I asked.

He chuckled, "At the top?" He sounded more than amused.

I felt like I spoke in hiker slang, even for hiker slang. And I wasn't sure why he was looking at me in such an odd way.

"I mean, are you thru- hiking from the north...from Canada?" I quickly corrected.

The man stared at me a few seconds, and said

"Yeah...yeah, I guess you could say I started from the top" He looked around and then over my shoulder, behind me, "Are you alone?"

His dark eyes narrowed on mine, and then he looked me over.

His eyes then met mine again.

"Um...yeah....I was wondering about the Sandy River crossing" I gulped, trying to hide my sudden uneasiness in his presence.

It felt as though he took an eternity to answer my simple question, and finally he replied, repeating my question with a question and then a strange answer.

"How is the river crossing?" He looked me over again, "Oh, its fine! You'll be fine until you reach the...oh...what is it called...the Javier crossing! That one is dangerous!" He said with a devilish grin.

I was a map reader. I had studied my maps front and back... I knew the names of all the river crossings by heart. JAVIER was not among them. Maybe the river he spoke of was in Washington. Maybe he was just trying to sound like he knew what he was talking about. Or maybe, maybe Javier was his name, and he was trying to be coy about how dangerous HE was.

I could feel my body reacting to my intuition. Every fiber of my being screamed "Get out of here!"

The world around me slowed down. I could hear my heart beat, and I felt my eyes dilate. I nodded, and said, "Ok, well... have a good hike!"

I practically blew through him to get passed. I walked as fast as I could without running away.

"Don't run!" I kept telling myself, as if he was a wild animal.

As soon as he was out of sight, I dropped my pack and dug out my gun and holster; attaching the holster back on to my hip belt. I loaded the five rounds of hollow point .38's and turned to look at the trail behind me.

My father in laws words rang in my ears, "Don't be afraid to shoot anyone!"

7. TRANSFORMATION

I had just a few miles to go to get to Big Lake Youth Camp. Every few steps I stopped to look over my shoulder. Was he following me? I practiced pulling my gun from its holster. It was hard as hell to do. The gun did not slip out easily. I double checked to make sure I still had my knife in my shorts pocket.

Movement on the trail behind me caught my eye, and I turned around to get a better look. Someone was coming towards me, and fast! I saw his dark hair first, and quickly scanned his gear, hoping it was not Javier. I clutched the grip of my gun in my right hand, still secured in its holster; I had a death grip on it. My chest felt like it was filling with hot water, and I could feel springs winding up in my hamstrings.

He was about fifty feet away, when he looked up at me from the trail. A warm wash of relief rushed over my body, and the wasted adrenaline made me tremble where I stood.

"Hey Data!" I called out with a shaky voice.

It was Data, the thru-hiker I met back in the lava fields. He had hitched a ride from the Lava Lake campground the evening we met, and spent a couple days in Bend.

"How are you doing?" he asked with a friendly smile.

We chatted for just a couple minutes before he jaunted down the trail ahead of me. Within a few minutes, more thru-hikers passed me by. All of them greeted me warmly as they passed. None of them were hikers I had met previously.

After an hour or so I caught up to all of them, sprawled around the trail in the shade, eating lunch. One girl offered me Sour patch Kids candy, but I kindly refused. It was one thing when people in town or day hikers offered me food; I found it hard to refuse it. But, when a long distance hiker offered me something, I felt like I was taking food from a starving refugee. The gesture was always appreciated, but I felt guilty to accept it.

I kept walking as the group finished their lunch. Also declining their invite to sit and eat with them. After thirty minutes or so I pulled up a seat on a large rock, and pulled out my maps. I was feeling confused about which way I needed to go to get to BLYC. The map showed an off trail veering to the left, leading to the camp.

The map also showed the PCT leading to a dirt road that would also take me to the camp. But, the Halfmile app notes said "do not take trail to the left". Data and the group passed me by, and I stopped them. "Are you guys taking the road or the trail to BLYC?"
Data replied, "You're going to want to take the trail to the left". And off they went. He was using Guthook's App.

It didn't take too much longer before I came across a small wooden sign that marked the trail to BLYC. I noticed an arrow drawn in the dirt, probably by the group of thru-hikers.
"Well," I thought, "I'm not that confused, but that is helpful, thanks!"

I took a moment to unload my gun, and repack it deep in my pack.

The short trail was dry, and the black dust stirred up around my ankles and calves. As I got closer to the youth camp I heard laughter, horses, and motorized boats. I was greeted by a large sign that said "WELCOME PCT HIKERS," (yep that's me) "PLEASE CHECK IN AT HEADQUARTERS." (Hmmm... I wonder where that is) "NO SMOKING...NO ALCOHOL...NO FIREARMS" (check...check...gulp).

A girl in a blue BLYC staff shirt found me coming off the trail and directed me to headquarters. Suddenly I was standing on the outskirts of a small A-framed community. She gave me the run down as we walked and other camp counselors led droves of pre-teens past us and around us to activities.
"There is a hiker area with plugs for electronics, and couches. You can pick up your resupply box, and organize your packs there. There are

laundry bins next to headquarters. If you need laundry done we will pick it up at one in the afternoon every day, and deliver it back to you by four." She said.

We stood on the steps of the Headquarters building, and she continued, "Dinner is served at six, and it is free unless you want to make a donation. Breakfast is at eight. The hiker camp areas are in the coves outside of camp, there's a map near the gift shop."
I kept thinking, "Is this place for real?"
Free hot food, showers, free camping, and laundry service? Maybe this is really a sweat-shop disguised as a youth camp.

I gave the camp employee my information and she went to retrieve my resupply box. I could have sent it all to Tianna's house. I had just left there that morning. But this was going to be my longest stretch between resupplies, and I figured the less I had to carry at any given time the better. I took my box over to the hiker area, and plopped down in the dirt near Data and the rest of the thru-hiker group.

Data came over to me and asked if he could weigh my pack. "That's why they call me Data, I am collecting data on all the hikers I meet this year; I'm writing an article when I'm done with the hike". He picked up my pack.
"It's kind of empty." I told him as if trying to impress him because I usually carried much more, as he connected his scale to my pack.
Data read, "39 pounds...and it is empty?" He laughed.
"What does yours weigh, full", I asked curiously.
"Usually about 29 pounds." He smiled.
"Sounds terrible." I said sarcastically.

But inside I was thinking how terribly heavy my pack was going to be. The resupply box I just picked up was my biggest one yet! I had packed it for six days, on top of what I had sent to myself in sisters (three days of food and other supplies). Ollalie Lake was not accepting resupply boxes. So, my next pick up wouldn't be until Timberline Lodge. An estimated seven days away.

Data and the group loaded back up.
"Well, have a good night Two-Sips!" he told me.
"We are trying to get in a fifty mile day today". And they were off like a heard of gazelles. To me, that really did sound terrible!

I put on my pack and then picked up my resupply box, and headed out to find a camping spot. It was 4:30, and I was looking forward to dinner. I wanted to clean up, make camp, resupply my pack, and be able to go right to sleep after dinner. As I walked through the camp, more campers and camp counselors passed me by.

The kids all looked so happy. The counselors sang songs, made jokes, and danced as they lead the campers. There was not one child who looked like they weren't having fun. Each of them on their way to do something exciting, I was sure. Boating, swimming, horseback riding, the possibilities were endless. For a moment, my inner child was envious. Then I started to feel guilty, and had wished desperately that my own son could experience something like this while he were younger.

"What is your dream vacation?" Charlie asked me as we spoke on the phone before we had met in person.
Charlie and I had met on an online dating site, a year after my first marriage ended in divorce.
"To take my son to Disney World!" I responded.
My son Cole was five by the time I had met Charlie.

I never did take my son on a Disney vacation. In fact, in the last ten years, we had taken very few family trips, and nothing like the ones I dreamed about. Charlie and I moved in together when Cole was seven. The next year I started attending college, while working full time. I believed in my heart that I was working towards something that would better our lives, and allow me to earn more money and time to take those vacations; to be able to give my son all the experiences I wished I could. Time passed, he kept getting older and the more I worked or went to school, the more I missed those opportunities. I finally had that Bachelor Degree, but no real family time memories. I became heavy with guilt; wondering if taking a month away from my family to complete this journey was too selfish of me.

Big Lake was beautiful. I followed its shore line, past a BMX dirt track, and through the trees. The water sparkled and lapped on the shore in the cove. I put my gear down on a flat area and walked down a path to sit at the edge of the water. Another place I wish my family could see.

I snapped some pictures with my phone and sent them to Charlie. I also sent a picture to Chris by text.
"If you haven't passed this place, you have to stop here!"

I wondered if they had gotten back on the trail yet, and if I'd ever see them again. I wondered how James' blisters were doing, and if his feet survived the lava fields.

Dinner time came and the campers filled the chow hall. The hikers all waited in line, and chit chatted among themselves. Most of them were south bound hikers, and none of them talked to me. And, for the first time on my hike, I didn't go out of my way to make friends. I sat down at a picnic table with a group of them, and devoured my grilled cheese sandwich and tomato soup, and an apple for dessert.

Two people came to sit down, and I recognized them from shelter cove. It was Haley and Road-Trip. Road trip had a large feather in his large brimmed floppy hat, and even though he already had a trail name, in my mind I called him "Yankee doodle". Haley's shins were bothering her, and they had been taking it slow. Haley was a ballerina who studied dance in New York City, before getting injured and moving back home to California.

I was glad to see their familiar faces, but I wasn't feeling like having much conversation. So, skipping seconds, I retreated to my tent and exploded my resupply box. I sorted through it, trying to get rid of anything I possibly could live without. Batteries, oatmeal, extra baby wipes, sunscreen, extra toothpaste, extra toilet paper, Anything! But no matter what I tried to discard, I knew my pack was going to still be heavy.

I laid in my tent and wished I was with Charlie having a beer with him at our favorite sports pub, Joe's. As I started to drift off I was startled awake to the sound of children and teens cheering. And then loud music. I unzipped my tent and looked around.

"Jesus, am I camping in the woofer?" I cursed under my breath.

Loud Christian rock ripped through the trees, the bass beat against my tent walls, and the kids sang along.

"Our God is an Awesome God!" They sang.

"Sleep is awesome. Sleep at nine o'clock at night on the PCT is especially awesome!" I growled.

But then I laid there and listened to the lyrics, and to how happy the kids and staff sounded singing together.

"Yeah, this is an awesome place. And I am on an awesome adventure. And thank you God for this amazing opportunity!"

I began to drift back asleep again, when I got a text message. It was Chris!

95

"We won't make it that far tonight. Maybe we will see you on the trail tomorrow."

I smiled, knowing my friends weren't that far behind me.

Day twenty-one

I woke later than normal, but still earlier than some of the other hikers. Many SOBO hikers had joined me in the camper's cove after dinner. I deflated my sleeping pad and rolled my sleeping bag as quietly as I could, being mindful not to wake others. It was a hard task since so much of my gear is made from noisy nylon.

I loaded everything in its perspective order, and stuffed my food bag in last, as usual. It was the heaviest thing in my pack. I was wishing I had Data's scale to weigh it. I bet it weighed a good six pounds or more! After loading the rest of my gear and strapping down my tent to the outside of my pack, I threw the pack over my right shoulder, and then on to my back.

"This thing has to weigh close to fifty pounds!" I thought, begrudgingly.

I had some good climbs to make. This was certainly the heaviest my pack had weighed since my first couple days, back when Charlie and I had first started. Back before we dumped all of our "just in case cause I'm afraid to die in the woods" gear. Charlie messaged me at 6:41AM, "You up bb?"

I followed the dirt road out of camp. I came to a parking area and turn around, and there I found the PCT trailhead. Following the trail, I walked past trees marked with cross country ski signs, and various overlapping dirt roads. Finally I came to the Mount Washington Wilderness boundary and crossed highway 20 near Santiam pass.

Near the trailhead at Santiam pass, I came across two large plastic tubs, and two folding chairs set up in the shade. Attached was a note "PCT trail magic for overnight section hikers, and thru-hikers."

I anxiously opened the tubs and found nothing but candy bar wrappers, and empty chip bags.

"Not like I needed anything extra…" I thought to myself.

I looked around, and the burnout seemed to go on for miles.

I thought about sitting for a few minutes in the chairs, just to have taken the opportunity, but hadn't been hiking long enough to justify it. However, I was highly disappointed that there weren't any salty snacks left in the tub: Knowing that junk food was still a few days away. The water jugs were also empty.

I had refilled my water back at a large pond just a few miles after BLYC. Even though I knew there weren't many water resupply points marked on the trail, I didn't carry more than two liters, because I was avoiding any more added weight.

My Halfmile map warned: WARNING! NORTHBOUND WATER ALERT NEXT WATER [KOKO LAKE] IN 12.9 MILES.

My goal for the day was to make it to Rock Pile Lake. If I got to there, I would have abundant water. But my total daily mileage would have to add up to 20 miles.

"I'm good for that." I coaxed myself as I walked.

"Besides, there are off trails along the way leading to other lakes in the area. If I run out of water, I can just take a detour for the day." At the time, I had no clue that most of these spur-trails were closed due to wild fire.

The forest around me had been taken out by wildfires in the years before. Small shrubs and saplings peaked out from the soft rich soil. The trail was dry and dusty. There was no shade, just warm sun beating down on me. I occasionally passed ponds, that weren't marked on my map. Their waters black, and lined with frothy slime.

I stopped at one to fill my water bottle. When I removed the Sawyer Squeeze water filter from the top of the bottle, the small white gasket fell on to the ground. I made an attempt to put in back in place, and filter my water. Unfiltered water spewed out from the edges of the filter, and into my water bladder.

"Shit!" I called out.

Again I removed the gasket, and replaced it; but it wasn't fitting correctly any more.

I still had a liter and a half of clean water. I could boil water later if I needed to. I also carried water treatment tabs. I could attach my filter directly to my water bladder line and surpass the need for the gasket. I tried to think of all the alternatives and contingency plans I had in place.

"There's a contingency plan for everything. You can figure it out!" I reassured myself.

I thought about alerting Charlie, and asking him to send me a new filter, but I wouldn't be able to get it until Timberline lodge, Days away. I was on my own for now, either way.

The thought also occurred to me that maybe Ollalie Lake would sell them in the general store. I made a mental shopping list: water filter, cheese burger, and a shower. I decided these were my new three survival essentials.

The incline of the trail wasn't steep but it was steady. I was finding this to be the nature of the Oregon PCT, a steady gradual incline, some drops, some flats, and then an incline. I also knew that these inclines often ended with some of the most beautiful views I had ever seen. I didn't mind the steady climbs any more. But, the weight of my pack and twenty days away from home started to get me down.

I messaged Charlie, "Man I get tired and sore quickly with extra weight!"

I had stopped more than usual to adjust my pack and put my feet up for a few minutes. The arches of my feet screamed at me with every step.

Charlie messaged me back, "And looks like you got a good incline. More breaks. Left, right repeat bb." He said.

Around 2 o'clock I found a large grouping of trees next to the trail, and placed my pack in the shade. I stood for a few moments, stretching and taking in the views around me. Burnout below on one side, and rolling thick forests on the other. The breeze tickled against my face and under my arms. Birds danced on air currents, and sang in the trees above me.

I closed my eyes and listened to the insects buzzing around me. Suddenly, I took pleasure in the aches and pains. My water filter didn't worry me. The weight of my pack meant I had more than enough food. I was overcome with faith that I would have all that I needed, and with that I could take care of myself. I had come a long way. I had made it a lot farther than my weaker-self thought I could do.

I mentally high-fived my stronger-self, "Yup, I told you so," said my stronger self!

I sat alone, taking it all in, And I took a picture of myself in the moment to document, "You don't want to forget her", I said to myself

"Think I'm gonna go 3.6 Miles and call it a day." I messaged Charlie.

That meant I wasn't going to make it to Rock Pile Lake today. But I was OK with that. There was a small pond and campsite I could make it to. And if the water wasn't sufficient there then I could push out the other four miles, if I HAD to.

Left, right. Left, right! I counted paces as I hiked.

The trail wound around a base of a large rock face. A day hiker headed south on the trail, as I stopped to take a couple pictures of it.

"Pretty impressive huh?" He said as he passed me.

The jagged rock looked like it could crumble down on top of me at any moment. It was big, and It was beautiful. But all I could really think was that I was going to have to get around it, and I had to keep walking UP to do it. Left...right...Left... Repeat...

The wind picked up as I got closer to what looked like "the top" of the incline. I kept my eyes on the trail in front of me, and set my gaze. If I stared too long at "the top" or the "finish", it felt like I was moving in slow motion. I wasn't paying attention, and suddenly a gust of wind hit me hard, and I almost fell over. I looked up and braced myself, trying to regain my balance. That's when I realized I had made it to the top, and was standing on the saddle.

In front of me was a vast green valley, and to the left a clear view of Mt. Jefferson in the distance. To my right stood the East Face of Three Fingered Jack. My mouth gaped, my knees became weak, and I uncontrollably burst into tears. I had seen many beautiful things on this journey, but this was by far the most magnificent sight to see, and what a surprise!

I held up my camera, and the wind gusts tried to knock it from my hands. I kept weeping. The wind blew my tears into my ears. I immediately realized the last time I had felt this way was the first time I held my son. I looked at him and cried uncontrollably. I was filled with joy and a love that I never had experienced until that moment.

In this moment, standing on the saddle, I was falling in love. I was filled with pure love for all that surrounded me, and I couldn't stop staring at it! I couldn't stop crying!

I quickly messaged Charlie, "this place is amazing!!! Tears!!"

He replied, "Awe bb. So happy for you!!!!!!"

But there were no real words to describe what had just happened to me, at the time. I stood for a while, taking pictures, as the wind knocked against me and threated to rip my phone from my hands. More than once, I adjusted my footing to keep from falling over.

I reluctantly decided it was time to keep going. The trail winded down steeply on a long series of switchbacks. I braced myself against the wind, and dug my poles into the soft trail with each step. Before too long I was walking through a burnout area again. The wind kept coming, and the white limbless charred trees rocked back and forth. I was going to have to camp soon, and I envisioned the wind blowing dead trees onto my tent at night; squishing me. When I reached my proposed camp sight, I left my pack against a fallen log to check out the nearby tiny pond.

The water was black, and full of decaying burnt logs. I stepped towards the water to get a better look and my boots sank in the black mud. I climbed up on some high rocks and gazed out around me. "There has to be something better". I thought to myself.
Leaving most of my gear behind, except for my knife and tracker, I scouted the area.

A large pond appeared after a quarter mile or so. The banks looked muddy, but they were flat, and the water looked clear. I returned to where I left my belongings, retrieved my gear, and returned to the large pond. Approaching my new campsite I stared up at the dead trees that surrounded the area. They stood tall and strait, as if they were standing guard over the pond. I chose a flat area near a large log, in hopes that if a tree were to fall on me in the night, the log would stop it from coming all the way down onto me.

As I made camp, two male hikers stopped to refill water on the other side of the pond. Judging by the size of their packs, I figured they were definitely section hikers, and probably a short section at that!

I sat and watched them. They waved, and I waved back; praying they weren't going to stay, because everything in me just wanted to be alone tonight. They soon left and I washed my socks while I waited for my dehydrated meal to re-hydrate.

Sitting half way out of my tent, I scooped the black bean chili into my mouth, and sipped on Mexican hot chocolate, enjoying the peace. Movement from the trail caught my eye. Something had walked from the trail, and was now slinking through the bushes. It was a dark tan color. I leaned forward to get a better look. It stopped, the black and white tipped ears flickered, and she raised her head. It was a doe.

I sat back a little farther into my tent, and stayed as still as I could. She walked towards me, now just fifty feet or so away. I felt the wind on my feet and concluded the wind was blowing towards me. Maybe she didn't know I was there yet? She walked delicately across the muddy banks and dropped her head at the water's edge; lapping up drink after drink.

Soon two more deer joined her at different spots around the pond. I quietly curled up in my sleeping bag, as the sun began to set, and fell asleep watching them take their time, disappearing back into the shrubs without a care in the world.

8. CLOSED FOR REHAB

A gust of wind knocked into my tent and startled me awake. I had fallen asleep with my tent door unzipped and rain fly open. I rubbed my eyes and peered out into the night sky. I realized, this was the first time I had seen the night sky while on my trip.

"Oh my god..." I whispered and I stretched my body out of the tent to get a better view of the sky around me.

There were more stars than I had ever seen in my entire life. Thick white swirls of stars clustered together. A shooting star dashed by, then another, and another. They glowed green and shot around in different directions. I closed my eyes, and whispered again, "ah Charlie, I miss you..."

I pulled my sleeping bag up around my ears and wished that Charlie was with me.

Day twenty-two

I dozed off again and woke once more startled by a wind gust. I laid looking out over the pond, just as the sun began to peak through the burnt trees. A fog rolled over the water, and glowed in the new sunlight. I felt too peaceful (not to mention sore) to rise with it. I drifted off, and awoke to my tracker beeping, incoming message.

It was Charlie, "you up bb?"

It was 6:19AM. I had over slept again! I repacked my gear slowly, and made some oatmeal and coffee. My socks were still wet from the washing the night before.

"Great!" I thought sarcastically, "Just what I need, more blisters". Wet socks and hiking do not mix well.

I finished lacing my boots and around 8AM I messaged my mom and Charlie from my tracker, "Off like a herd of turtles!"

Charlie responded, "a bad ass turtle."

I laughed and shook my head. Time to walk.

I could see Wasco Lake below me as I hiked away from my pond near Koko Lake. Charlie and I had spent some time exploring the Wasco lake area via google earth. It was definitely steep terrain to get to the lake, and I was glad I didn't have to depend on it for water. The water looked blue and serene, but the climb back to the trail would have been hellish!

I passed Rock Pile Lake, and saw the two male hikers packing up camp. We waved at each other again, but I didn't stop to chat. The trail was going to be fairly easy today, equally uphill and downhill, and somewhat level. I planned on a twenty mile day today. I had to be sure to keep a good pace, and not take too many rest periods, so that I could make camp at a decent hour again. I was starting to really count on having a quiet hour or two before sleep to regroup, look over maps, and have a nice meal before falling asleep. It seemed to make the next day go more smoothly.

Soon, I had a great view of Mt. Jefferson in the close distance. "I'll be there in a few hours or so!" I thought.

The mountain looked Marvelous. "Helooooo Mr. Jefferson!" I said out loud and waved my arms with my trekking poles in hand.

As I got closer and closer to Mt Jefferson, the terrain around me began to change back to familiar "getting closer to a volcano" terrain (I'm sure there is a geologist out there that could tell me what it is really called). Dusty black trail, granite, shale, and one particular flower I hadn't seen since Charlie and I were hiking together a couple days before Crater Lake.

I call it a "Who-Ville flower". I stopped and said hello to it, and pet its furry wig-like top.

"Hi Charlie." I whispered to it. As if it could telepathically send the message to him.

As it turns out this flower does have a name! It is called the Pasque Flower. After some research once I returned home, I learned that this plant has been used medicinally for many years to treat things such as anxiety, headache, and depression. But please, consult a real botanist before taking my word for it! Regardless, I thought the plant was a powerful motif for my journey.

I took a moment to remember how wonderful it was that Charlie and I were able to do some of this journey together, and I felt excited to know that we would have more adventures to plan.

"We make a kick ass team!" I smiled.

I reached the top of another hill, and pulled up a burnt log. It was lunch time. I took off my socks (that were still damp) and laid them on a rock in the sun. I sat, barefoot after taking off my boots to let my blisters breathe, scooping peanut butter with a Snickers bar, when the two male hikers crested. They stopped.

"How you guys doin?" I asked with a mouth full of peanut butter and Chocolate.

"Great! How'd that campsite work out for you last night?" one of them asked, "That wind was crazy" he continued.

"Yeah, woke me up a few times..." I replied, sounding like I didn't care .

"Did you see the stars?" I asked with more excitement.

"Yeah, it is pretty out here. I'm from Jersey. My name is Jared. This is Moritz". He pointed to his friend.

"Helllllooo", He said and nodded at me. "I'm Moritz." He had a strangely familiar accent.

"He's from Germany." Jared said.

"You can call me Two-sips...I'm from Oregon", and I offered a fist bump. I didn't shake hands out here. I wasn't sure how much hand sanitizer anyone was using, and we were all a bit on the petri-dish side of clean.

"How far are you going?" Jared asked.

"Bridge of the Gods" I said, "I started in Ashland. You?" I asked, as I looked over their gear. I had become one of "those" people...

"Probably up to Timberline, we started yesterday at highway 20". Jared replied.

They soon started back on the trail. I took a few minutes to put on my almost dry socks, and gather up my belongings. I was hoping the two would get a good enough start in front of me that I could camp alone again for the night.

After a couple more hours I reached Shale Lake. I needed to refill my water. Approaching the lake, just off the trail, I saw Moritz and Jared stopped there too, across the body of water from me. Shale Lake was more like a large pond, and it reeked of deer piss. But, the view of Mt. Jefferson was beautiful!

"Another snack won't hurt!" I told myself, and sat down on the mossy bank, unknowingly placing my hand in a pile of deer droppings. "Crap!" I shuttered, "Literally!"

I took out my water bottle, and drank directly from the filter. It was no longer leaking! But, movement from inside my water bottle caught my eye. I held it closer to get a better look. Tiny red shrimp like organisms darted around in the water that I had been drinking since the pond near KoKo lake! Without thinking, I opened the bottle and poured the contents into Shale Lake. And then I gasped!

"Way to go smarty pants...You probably just introduced an invasive species into the water, and the area will be condemned soon!"

I walked about ten feet down the shoreline, and refilled my bottle. Looking closely at it to make sure there were no weird little animals in it this time. I looked over my map, it was just after 3PM and I still had seven miles to go.

The trail started to make a steady decent. I found myself jogging along, you know, taking advantage of the downhill. Then again it had taken me almost three hours to cover five miles. I was not moving fast or steady. I was exhausted! I was quickly approaching Milk Creek, and could hear the waters rushing in the near distance. I figured I could just camp next to the creek, and still be able to get up and leave early enough in the morning to cross Russell Creek.

The colder temperatures in the higher elevations at night would freeze parts of the glacier. I wanted to get to Russell Creek early because it was glacier fed. The earlier in the morning that I crossed it, the lower the water would be. If I could cross before the sun began warming the southern slopes, I'd be golden!

My hopes and dreams of making camp by Milk Creek and having a timely dinner were shattered. A large family was already camping next to the creek, taking up the camping area. I sat down in the rocks, and puffed on my electronic cigarette, while I contemplated my next move. It was already after 6PM. My initial planned stopping point was only two more miles away.

I had already covered eighteen miles, what the hell is two more? I stood to put my pack on, and my aching neck exploded in fiery pain. I took a deep breath, crossed the rushing creek, and made my way back up the trail; with a seven-hundred foot elevation climb over the next mile. The trail disappeared underneath thick over grown wild blueberry bushes. I could hear voices coming from the brush and stopped to scan the area.

Haley and Road Trip had found a flat area to set up camp for the night. I watched them from the trail for just a moment, deciding whether or not I wanted to invite myself over. I quickly decided against it, and chose to continue to the pond. I walked away quietly, and they never saw me.

Just after 7PM I rounded a corner and saw part of a large pond. "Oh thank you God, I made it!" I thought.

I took a few steps more and then stopped dead in my tracks. Blinking, I stared at a figure in the water.

"Is that a naked man?" I thought to myself while my eyes locked on the figure in front of me. .

He was at least one hundred feet away.

"More importantly, is that a naked Jared?"

Before I could turn away, I heard a German voice say, "Hellllloooo". I turned towards the voice.

Oh My GOD, there stood Moritz, about twenty feet away from me. He had been watching me, watching Jared (trying to figure out if it was a naked Jared). And as soon as Moritz had said Hello, Jared turned around, saw me and shouted "OH MY GOD I'M SO SORRY"!! He tried to cover himself with a red handkerchief, and quickly dipped down in the water.

"NO! NO!" I shouted back waving my arms around as if to shew him away, quickly turning my back to him, mortified!

"YOU'RE FINE!", I yelled, and I instantly regretted saying that.
"NO! I DIDN'T MEAN IT LIKE THAT!" I yelled in a panic, trying to back pedal.

I made a beeline for some nearby bushes, still shouting.
"IS THERE ANOTHER CAMPSITE? I'M JUST GONNA CAMP BACK HERE!" and I crashed my way through the shrubs.

Luckily, there was a large campsite concealed by the bushes. I plopped my pack in the dirt and started laughing uncontrollably.

After I had camp set up, I realized I was going to need more water to cook dinner. Moritz and Jared were camped and hanging out at the only accessible area. I walked over, "Can I get some water?" Why was I asking their permission?

"Of course! And You're welcome to join us for coffee!" Jared invited. I thanked him for the invite, and submerged my water bottle.

"Hey, Two-sips, do you hang your food?' Jared asked me.

"Nope!" I said shortly, while I watched the water slowly flow into my water bottle. I turned back to look at Jared, "It is my pillow", and I grinned at him.

"But I'll shoot anything that comes near my tent", I smiled bigger. He looked at me blankly.

"Hey, sorry about earlier…" he said sheepishly.

"Seriously," I responded, "I've seen my husband naked like over one-thousand times!" I laughed. I blushed a little.

"I think I'm going to go have dinner and go to bed" I said. Moritz chuckled through sipping his coffee.

It didn't take long for me to drift off to sleep before I woke to loud crashing in the bushes nearby. I sat up and felt around for my gun. I stopped and listened harder. The sun was still trying to set. I unzipped my tent slowly, and poked my head out. It kept crashing, limbs shaking, leaves crackling. It sounded like something large was jumping. I glanced towards the men's campsite, and didn't see any movement.

I got up, out of my tent, with hopes to get a look at what was making such a ruckus. About thirty feet away, the top of a small tree bent back and then swung strait up. I saw Jared pulling on a rope and raising a food bag into the tree on like a pulley.

"Dick!", I thought to myself, irritated that he was hanging their food bag so close to my campsite.

Then I laughed at my irritation! I was the one who slept with food in my tent, and it usually rested under my head. In fact, I kept my trash bag at my feet at night as well. So, it wasn't really fair of me to be so irritated at Jared. I knew where the bear would want to sniff out first, given the choice. I just thought it was inconsiderate of him to hang the bag so close to me. Maybe he thought my chances were better since I was the one packing a gun.

Day twenty-three

The morning came quickly, and without any bear intrusions during the night. I had a little over two miles to go before I would reach Russell Creek. Turning on my tracker, I sent out a message to let everyone know back home that I was starting the day at 6:40AM: "High Ho Silver Away!" I wrote.

My mom later chimed in, "Ha Ha! Carry on Lone Ranger!! Lots of love".

I could hear the rushing waters of Russell Creek nearby. I was feeling nervous about having to cross the water alone. All that I knew about it was that it was cold glacier water, and was considered to be a dangerous crossing on the Oregon PCT.

"You made it across the Sandy River, You'll be just fine!" I reassured myself. I looked around for a raven, but I was definitely alone on this one.

The creek came into view below, as the trail descended towards it. "Really?", I thought, "That is it?"

The rushing water echoing in the canyon sounded much more intimidating than the flow appeared. I made my way to the banks and realized that the waters were probably deeper than they let on, and the creek was moving fast.

The good thing was I had made it to the creek early, before 8:00am. The water was lower than it would be by this afternoon. Worst case scenario, If I did fall in, I may not get swept away, but I would be wet and cold or twist an ankle. Hit my head on a rock… drown…

I decided to walk up stream about fifty or sixty feet to see if there was a better area to cross. I selected a section that looked like there were large and flat enough boulders to step on, and jump across. I unbuckled my backpack, and clipped my tracking device to the waist of my rain pants. I slid my knife into my shirt pocket, and buttoned it closed.

Using my trekking poles to test the stability of the first boulder, I then stepped onto it. I pierced the icy waters with my poles between boulders to estimate the depth. I measured about twelve inches. It was most definitely deeper than I thought. Digging my poles between two rocks, I leaped to the next boulder. It was slick with slime, and my left foot slid. I pushed myself forward on my poles so my pack wouldn't pull me backwards. Regaining my balance, I made the last few leaps to the other side of the bank.

After backtracking to the trail, I sat down to have a snack and message Charlie.

"Made it safe across Russell Creek!"

He soon responded, "Way to go baby! High-five!"

Charlie's unwavering support and encouragement had brought me a long way on this trip.

"You on a mission today?" He asked.

"Everyday", I snickered as I typed the message back to him.

"Mission today is Cheetos and a Pepsi at Olallie!" I said.

"Holy Shit! You gonna make it to Olallie today?" Charlie asked.

A sense of pride spewed deep from my soul and out of my fingertips, "Yes sir I will, two days early!"

We exchanged messages as I hiked along. After PCT mile 2029, the trail made a steady thirteen-hundred foot climb over the next few miles. The climb was more gradual as I entered into Jefferson Park, and then it leveled out for a bit.

The park was lovely. The surrounding landscape opened up into meadows with short shrubs, conifers, and small wild flowers. As I walked I passed various, well-kept, spur trails that lead to surrounding lakes and camping areas. Mt. Jefferson was now to my back, but the view of it was nonetheless breathtaking here.

Some of the spur trails were closed due to degradation and over use. The park officials were making a great effort to rehabilitate the areas, and to keep the park in pristine condition. I kept passing signs, "Closed for Rehab".

What a coincidence, I too, in some way, was also closed for rehab. Amy Winehouse lyrics filled my head and I hummed along as I walked.

I compared my journey to the closed trails and the efforts being made to rehabilitate the Jefferson Park area. The irony was that I didn't come out here to heal by protecting myself. I came out here to suffer. To deprive myself of luxuries; things like electricity, internet, grocery stores, daily hot showers, fast food, booze. I came out here to learn to take care of myself. To maybe get lost, and find my own way. I wanted to feel trampled on and broken down; I wanted to know surrender.

A few months before my hike, I sat in my doctor's office, sobbing. "Do you think you are depressed?" The Nurse Practitioner asked me sympathetically.

"No, I just need coping skills!" I started laughing through my tears, and wiping snot from my red nose.

"How much do you drink?" She asked me

"Usually? About a bottle of wine every night. I mean, sometimes just a couple glasses!" I put my hands up as if trying to hold her off or convince her. But the truth was closer to a bottle every night. And if there was anything else, I would drink that too.

"How long has this been a regular habit for you?" She asked, with her head cocked to one side, handing me the box of tissues.

What was I supposed to say? I had been going to the same Doctor for several years, and I felt so embarrassed to be having this discussion!. I focused my thoughts to more recent years, " I don't know, maybe since 2013?"

"I don't sleep at night without a few drinks!" I continued.

And that was true. I was plagued by insomnia, and anxiety.

I had gone to the doctor that day because I was having a lot of chronic pain in my abdomen, and I was afraid that my liver or pancreas were suffering. Subconsciously, I wanted help; but I never asked for it outwardly. She agreed to run some tests for me.

"When you're ready to stop drinking, we can help you with an outpatient program." She told me.

I left the trail and sat in the shade of some small trees, and ate peanut butter; contemplating my life choices. Haley and Road Trip came down the trail. Haley hobbled. I could tell that one of her legs was really bothering her. She stepped, and then bounced off her tippy-toes on the other foot. We exchanged hellos, and remarked how gorgeous the park was. Then they continued on.

Soon Jared and Moritz came by, and waved. We all bounced around each other for much of the day, but never really hiked together or spoke much.

It wasn't long before I crossed the northern boundary of the park, and the trail began to climb into the forest. Day hikers passed. I stood breathless on the side of the trail and let them by. I kept going up. Slowly. The trail came to a large open area, and disappeared over a rocky hill. I once again set my gaze on the path ahead, about ten feet in front of me, and marched. My tracker beeped with an incoming message, but I didn't stop to read it. I was in pain, fatigued, and it was hot. Stopping was not an option.

When I crested the hill I was amazed by the view before me. A barely visible trail etched its way through miles of jagged rock and boulders. In the distance I got my first good look at Mt. Hood.

I smiled ear to ear, "Jesus, I can almost see the end of my trip from here!" I realized.

Today was the twenty-third of July. It was still hard for me to fathom how much ground I had covered and how long I had been away from home.

I made my way down the rocky trail, and I could see Haley and Road Trip ahead of me a couple hundred yards. Soon they disappeared from sight. I began to notice spur trails in the rock field, leading away in every direction. I reluctantly turned on my phone to use my Halfmile app, to keep track of whether or not I was actually on any trail at all.

I stopped and clambered up on a large boulder, and laid in the sun. I messaged Charlie, "Will you call Holly and make a hair appointment for me, for when I'm home?"

I laid there and listened to the chipmunks squeak and run about, for almost forty five minutes
After a while of more walking, I came to an unpaved road, and noticed Haley sitting in the shade across from me. She laid in the dirt with one leg propped on her pack. I walked over to her.

"Do you need help?" I asked as I got closer to her.

"No," She said, "Jon just went to see if anyone camping at Britenbush Lake campground could give us a ride to Olallie... I can't walk on my leg."

I offered her some ibuprofen, but she declined. It wasn't working for the pain any longer.

"Well, do you want a Vicodin?" I asked her.

I dug out my first aid kit, and handed her one of the three Vicodin I had packed, just in case I had to drag myself to help with a broken leg or something. She took the pill, but reluctantly.

I sat down with her in the shade. I didn't feel right leaving her there. After ten minutes or so, a red SUV came up the dirt road. Road Trip had successfully returned with a rescue crew of strangers.

"You should come with us!" Haley said to me.

I thought about it, as the hot sun beat down on the back of my neck.

"No, it is not part of my trip." I said.

But I wasn't sure what I really meant.

"I've got another six miles, I'll see you guys there!"

111

Road Trip loaded Haley's gear into the SUV, and they all waved goodbye as they made a U-turn, and drove away.

The rest of the day seemed to go on forever. At times I was dragging myself up hills, jogging down hills, and walking methodically near rocky cliffs. I wanted desperately to be done for the day, and to be gorging myself on junk food at Olallie Lake Resort. I hurt more today than any other day since I had started, especially my feet and lower back.

Charlie urged me to take it easy, and he wondered if my new insoles were to blame.
"No!" I responded, "I think my feet are very pissed that I get up and carry 40Lbs for fifteen to twenty miles every day for last twenty two days!" I meant to be snarky.

I started kicking myself for not accepting the ride when I had the chance.

I was taking another break around 4:00PM, when Jared and Moritz came down the trail. I sat in the dirt on the side of the trail, in the shade.
"Hey!" Jared greeted me, "Stopping for dinner?"
I glanced up from my map, "No, just taking a look at the last few miles ahead of us."

We had just under three miles left to go, and I could see that the trail was about to make one last good climb, before dropping down to Olallie Lake.
"Looks like it is all downhill from here!" I grinned at them jokingly, not divulging what I really knew, but assuming they had also been reading their maps.

Jared and Moritz smiled, and took off. I wasn't sure if they knew I was kidding.

I reached the "Many Lakes View Point", and took a moment to look out over the valley below. I stared at the lakes below me, and thought about the large meal I would get at Olallie Lake Resort. I had checked their website while planning my stops, prior to leaving Ashland. I wasn't going to be able to send a resupply box there, but there was a general store. I thought about Shelter Cove and the amenities they had, and figured it would be comparable.

Worst case scenario, I could get a hot microwaved meal, take a shower, and because I was two days ahead of schedule I would take an unplanned zero day to rest. I needed to rest. All of the miles were finally starting to take a toll on my body. My hips burned as I walked, and I was beginning to get a large blister on the heel of my right foot. My body was begging and pleading with me to take it easy.

The last two miles were downhill, and I thought that would be easier than going up. However, every step down the shale path was grueling. Pain shot from the bottoms of my feet, up my legs, and into my hips. I kept stopping to bend forward on my trekking poles, with hopes to take some pressure of my lower back and hips. My pack no longer fit me correctly, "You should have taken it to the REI in Bend to get fitted for a new waist belt" I scolded myself.

Two young men were coming down the trail, and I stepped to the side so they could pass. They were thin, wore cotton t-shirts and board shorts, and carried day packs that were busting at the seams. A little terrier type dog ran between them, and yapped at me as they got closer.

One of them stopped and asked, "Where did you camp last night?"

It took a moment for me to answer. Trying to remember was hard because of the inner dialog I was having with my throbbing feet and hips, but I wanted to be polite.

"Um, I don't think it has a name... A pond, about fifteen or sixteen miles south." I finally answered.

Both of their mouths dropped open. "Oh my gosh, are you hiking the PCT?" One of them asked.

The other chimed in, "Yeah, are you like that Wild lady?"

This question was not an original. I had been asked it by friends, family, co-workers, and strangers on and off the trail...

"No, I am not like that Wild lady..."I rolled my eyes and forced a smile.

"But I am hiking the Oregon section of the PCT." I said.

"That's cool!", the first one said.

"I'd love to do something like that", the second young man said enviously.

The two of them asked me questions about the logistics of planning a long distance hike before they released me back to the trail.

Finally on mostly level ground, I noticed a piece of paper stuck to a tree. It said "WELCOME PCT HIKERS". A short description of how to get to Olallie Lake resort was hand written on the note. I followed the directions, passing the old ranger's cabin, and made my way through a grove of trees and to the parking area of the store. I stood there looking around, and my heart sank.

"Two-Sips, you are not getting a hot meal OR a shower here.." The realization brought me to a new kind of all-time low. As I approached the main building, which was the general store, a man and a woman were setting up a large Coleman stove on a picnic table. I walked past and they called out to me,
"Hey! We are going to make some hot dogs if you want any!"

All I could think was that I must look VERY homeless for complete strangers to be offering me a meal. I smiled and said thank you as I made my way up the rickety stair way and porch that led into the store.

Inside, the wood flooring creaked underfoot. I looked around. There were no lights on, but the space was lit up by the sunshine through the windows. My nostrils filled with the smell of old wood and dust as I entered. A young woman sat behind the small counter near the register, and she smiled at me. Her long auburn hair draped softly around her pale thin face.

"Hi", I said through a smile and closed teeth. I scanned the shelves around me. No hot food. No microwave. No lights. I walked to the back of the store, and found two refrigerators with handwritten price lists. I opened the fridge, and grabbed a Pepsi. The cold can burned in my hand, and I held it to my forehead and rolled it down my cheek as I made my way back to the front of the store.

On my way to the counter I grabbed a bag of Cheetos and a can of chili.
"Do you have a can opener?" I asked the girl with the auburn hair.
She rang me up for my snacks, and opened the can of chili for me.
"If you're a PCT hiker," she said, "You can camp for free in the day use area...There are tables up there too!", she said kindly.

I had a lot of questions, specifically about showers and recharging my battery pack, but I had a feeling I already knew the answers.
"Thank you!", I gathered the food up in one arm.
"I'll be back for some other things...Right now I am going to go be very unladylike like with this chili!", I giggled as I walked out of the store.

I passed the couple who were making hot dogs, and made my way to the day area. I grabbed the first picnic table I came across, and plopped down. I guzzled the first half of my Pepsi, and then tore open the bag of Cheetos, stuffing a small handful into my mouth. I dug out my titanium spoon from my pack, and contemplated heating the chili in my jet boil.

"Nah, it'll just make a mess!", I concluded, and shoveled the thick cold bean slop into my mouth right out of the can.

It was 5:30pm and I message Charlie, "Made it".

Soon he responded, "I hope they have a burger waiting for you!"

I ate handfuls of Cheetos as I typed my reply, "No, definitely more run down than expected...There goes my shower dreams...I am hoping they even have a plug in for my charger!"

I set up my tent, and tucked my gear away, before returning to the store to ask where I could find an outlet.

More hikers had arrived, and were crowded around the couple who had offered me a hot dog.

"There is still food left!", the woman called out to me.

Jared and Moritz sat nearby, swallowing down hot dogs. Haley and Road Trip were also there. And a few other faces that I didn't recognize, but all of them hikers. It soon dawned on me that these people weren't feeding the homeless, they were trail angels!

I made my way back into the store, and went to the refrigerator to grab a beer. The girl with the auburn hair still sat at the front counter. She smiled at me as I placed my battery pack and charging cord on the counter and dug money out of my Ziploc wallet.

"Is there a place that I can plug my things in to recharge?" I asked, afraid to hear the answer.

"There is no power," she said, "But we have a car battery hooked up to a inverter... I can charge your things for a little while." and she kindly took my battery pack. I returned outside to join the rest of the hikers.

It didn't take long before the hikers had completely taken over the front area of the store. Twinless and her sister Balbosa (SOBO hikers), Mystery, Road Trip, Haley, Jared, Moritz, a couple form Ireland who were hiking a large portion of Oregon, and a young woman from Alaska. We gathered around, sharing stories about our hike, and laughing at each other's discomforts, lack of hygiene, and how we all got our trail names.

"And then she says, it's all downhill from here!" Jared shared details of our last conversation from the trail that day, "And pretty soon it dawned on me... and I said to Moritz, I think she was just fucking with us!"

We laughed like old friends who had known each other for years. I soon forgot all about my charging worries, and the fact that I hadn't showered in four days. It happened to be Moritz's birthday, so we all sang to him and passed around a bag of Oreos to celebrate.

After the trail angels treated us to bacon s'mores next to the lake, I retreated to my tent to lay down and look over my maps. It was almost 9 o'clock, and the sun was beginning to set. I messaged Charlie to let him know I was turning in for the night.

"Doing the math on you & such. You should just do 15's lol" Charlie said in his message, "You have 104 miles left!"

I was shocked.

I knew I had come a long way, and I knew I was nearing the end of my trip, but I still hadn't done the math yet.

"What?", I responded, "I can be DONE in just five days!" (Almost ten days ahead of my original plan). I laid there, contemplating if I would continue on the next day, as planned. I could buckle down and just get the whole thing done and over with in no time at all. Five days was NOTHING!

I began to think about how badly I wanted to be home. Maybe I could just take the morning off, and do a nero day (nearly a zero day).

I messaged Charlie again, "love you babe. Going to sleep. Not starting in morning. Will msg when up."

I laid in my tent, listening to the sounds of the morning. It was barely light out, but I could hear the sounds of a few hikers starting to pack. I stayed still, rubbing my legs and hips. I wiggled my toes, they were even stiff. I sat up and dug out my ibuprofen. Suddenly, the all too familiar sensation of menstrual cramps filed my lower abdomen. "Great", I thought, "No wonder I have been so tired, and my hips have been hurting so badly."

Laying back down I rested my hands just below my belly button, and took in a deep breath. I smiled. Generally, a woman is only grateful to have her period after a very frightening unexpected or unwanted pregnancy scare. Trust me! It is the longest week or two of your life, waiting for that first cramp! But this time was a gentle reminder to be grateful for this magical, feminine body that was mine. And you have to be a woman to understand, but, it is important to know that usually the things that make us appear to be weak, actually make us stronger. I was hiking the trail, solo, living out my dreams, in all my feminine glory!

Day twenty-four

I laid in my tent until almost nine o'clock in the morning. I was contemplating if I should stay another day at Olallie Lake. I was ahead of schedule, my body was begging me to rest, and my battery pack had hardly any charge on it. It kept getting unplugged to share the car battery with other hikers.

I messaged Charlie, "Might stay one more night but don't want to". He urged me to stay. Timberline Lodge was going to be my last resupply point, and was the closest place for power. It was fifty-four miles away.

I took my battery charger and cord back into the store, where the kind auburn-haired girl connected it to the car battery for me. I went back out to my picnic table to have coffee and oatmeal. I looked over my maps, and decided that if I did 20 mile days, I could make it to Timberline in two and a half days. Maybe I could rent a nice room and take a bubble bath. Maybe I would order room service. Ahhh... Bubble bath...

By 11 o'clock, the trail angels were back in camp, setting up their stoves to make everyone hot dogs again.

I messaged Charlie, "Trail angels are back with hot dogs and candy. I guess I'll stay. Lol!"

The other hikers and I gathered around, and helped ourselves to the cooler of beers and soda. A tall man with a long white beard came into the camp, he was a thru-hiker and introduced himself as "Toasted Toad". The crowd of hikers greeted him, and he checked out the scene. "I'm just passing through, still have ten or fifteen miles to cover for the day!" He said.

After some conversation, Haley and I proceeded to tell him all about the trail angel offerings.

"Last night they made us bacon s'mores, and later they are going to make nachos!" Haley told him.

"Yeah, and they have beer!" I added.

Eventually, we talked him into staying.

For hours I sat in the camp area, surrounded by other hikers who shared stories and we had more laughs. I was feeling grateful. It felt like I was in a dream most of the day, or maybe it was the beers... The Angels brought out the nacho bar, and we commenced to fill our bellies again. More hikers hobbled in and made their way to the nacho bar and cooler.

"There are section hikers and there are LASHER's", Toasted Toad was giving a lesson on PCT hiker lingo.

"A LASHER," he explained, "is a long ass section hiker".

Well, maybe I am a lasher.. I thought to myself.

"Lashers hike five-hundred miles or more…" he said with an almost southern drawl.

Oh…That is not me..

"I think four-hundred or more miles counts as a long ass distance" I loudly disputed.

"Nope, gotta go five-hundred or more!" Toasted Toad rebutted.

"Well maybe I'll just keep going once I get to Washington", I laughed, "So I can be part of the silly LASHER club".

One thing I don't understand is the titles we put on ourselves or on others, and why this is so important to us; especially out here! It didn't really matter how far we were going, or where we came from, but it was one of the biggest conversation topics on the trail. I wasn't out here to win any freaking trophies. So, it pissed me off that I cared at all!

The yellow jackets had started to swarm the food table. Some of the hikers bolted to the edges of the camp area, others swatted at the bees and covered their food.

"It's OK, they don't want you, they want your food." I said softly to one of the hikers sitting next to me. I separated out some meat to the edge of my plate.

"Watch", I said.

A yellow jacket landed on my plate, and after inspecting the food, went to the meat. It gathered up a small amount of ground beef, rolling it into a ball under its thorax, and took off with it; the way a helicopter carries a water bucket. I helped cover the food on the table, and then set out a small portion of meat away from the crowd. Soon, the majority of the bees had found the meat, and were leaving the hiker's food alone.

"You're a god damn bee whisperer!" Joked one of the hikers.

Soon, familiar faces made their way into camp.

"Holy hell!" I shouted, and jumped out of my seat.

"Look what the mountain lion drug in!"

It was Chris and James!

"Oh God, not you again" James joked, "I thought we had lost her", he said to Chris.

Chris and James had been a day or so behind me since I left Big Lake Youth Camp, and I hadn't seen them since Shelter Cove. It was good to see their smiling faces, and feel the gut laugh induced by James' witty sense of humor. They were only passing through, but stayed to have nachos and a soda.

After dinner I sat down at my picnic table and attempted to make a daily plan for the remainder of my hike. It was important that Charlie knew EXACTLY when I planned on making it to the Bridge of the Gods. He had taken certain days off from work to make the drive to pick me up, and I needed to be spot on. James and Chris sat down at the table and inquired about what I was doing.

"Making a plan...reading maps...It's almost time to go home", I said with a lump in my throat.

"Ah, plans shlams", James scoffed and laughed. "I don't even know where we are going everyday", he said, "I've just been following this guy around the woods for the last three weeks", he laughed and pointed at Chris.

"Yeah, I think I should have done this before I had four beers", I joked.

Chris checked out my new tent, "This is NICE!", He said, "Way better than that crappy green tarp you were lugging around!"

Chris and James had decided it was time for them to head out, and get to their next camp spot a few miles down the trail. Although I was bummed to see them go again, it was easier this time. I was a different person than the girl they had left at Shelter Cove. We hugged, and high-fived.

"Maybe we'll see you at Timberline", said Chris. And they hiked away.

My charger had been in the store for the majority of the day. I went in to get it, and buy myself one more beer. The girl handed me the battery pack and said, "I think there is something wrong with your charger. I keep plugging it in, but it won't stay on".

I pushed the power button on the charger, three of the five bars lit up.

"Shit", I thought. I was planning on doing short hiking days to not only be easy on my body, but to make sure Charlie and I landed in Cascade Locks at the same time.

"Thank you so much for charging it for me", I said to the girl and returned outside.

"The trail angels are making s'mores by the lake", said Toasted Toads joining me at my picnic table, where I was draining my blisters. He handed me some Band-Aid blister pads.

"You want to take good care of those heels", he said to me with a kind smile.

"Thank you" I said and took the bandages.

"I saw you up here messing with them, thought you might need these", he added. Toasted Toad's eyes smiled with warm kindness. He was a hard core hiker, and an outdoors man, but he had a gentle soul that lit up his entire being.

"Thanks again. I think I am going to skip s'mores tonight and head to bed".

"Oh sure", he responded. "Lure me in with beer and food, and then not stay for the party!" He joked with me.

"I know! Trail Dancer (Haley, now given a trail name by Toasted Toad) and I are totally the Sirens of Olallie Lake", I laughed, "Stop hiking... Come, we have beer and nachos!" I said coaxingly, swirling my hands above my head. We snickered, and I said goodnight as he made his way to the lake shore for s'mores.

What he didn't know is I was struggling with the amount of drinks I had that day. I was scolding myself inside. I knew if I returned to the lake, I would surely drink more; ruining my hiking ability for the next day or more.

And completely ruining my renewed sense of normal.

9. BEE-AWARE

Day twenty-five

By morning, the trail angels were back with loafs of bread, homemade cherry jam, and hard boiled eggs. All before most of us were up and moving. Toasted Toad was already packed up and came by my camp spot before heading out. The trail angel, Broken-Leg, was setting up the breakfast spread at the picnic table in my camp area. I was up by 5:30 in the morning, and by the time they got there I had just stuffed the last of my gear into my bag.

"I think I have time for a small meal", I said graciously.

I wrote my email down on a piece of paper for Broken-Leg. His wife was planning on hiking the Oregon section next summer.

"Please let me know what I can do to help! You both have been so wonderful, I'd like to repay the favor." I said, handing him the paper.

After the generous breakfast, I refilled my water bladder from a hose that was available to hikers behind the store. I made my way back to the old ranger cabin, and started back on the trail where I had left off two days before. It was almost 7:00am.

It was cold and windy, overcast and slightly gloomy. I crossed an unpaved road, and walked under massive power lines. I passed Jude lake. My next water supply would be Lementi Creek, roughly ten miles after leaving Olallie. I tracked Toasted Toad as I went along, to pass the time.

The trail dipped down, lowering in elevation. It wasn't long before the trail followed a large creek bed, and I checked my map after estimating my mileage. I was walking through the Lementi spring bed, and it was dry. I sat down to have a snack, and check my water. I had two liters. I would be fine, and I could refill at Trooper Spring, just up the trail.

Normally in these weather conditions I wouldn't worry so much about only having two liters of water. But, this was the first spring I had come to that was bone dry. My next camp site was still almost ten miles away, and after that it was another ten miles or so before another "spring" popped up on my Halfmile notes. I needed to make sure I had one good water resupply, just in case the other springs were dry.

In hardly any time I came across the trail junction to Trooper Spring. It was well marked with a wooden sign, and I took the spur trail to the left. The weather was turning colder, and it felt like rain was on the way. The brush was wet, and my fingers turned cold while pushing aside the overgrown brush. I came to a small campsite, and it looked as though it had been used with in the last day or two.

"Maybe this is a good sign the spring will be running", I thought.

I came to an open marshy area. Tall grasses and stubby brush filled in a large wetland area. To my right was an overgrown creek bed, with hardly any flowing water. To my left was a very small pond, that was deep with water. But the water was black, and it had a foul looking layer on it. There were boards in the water; an old walkway, maybe. A rotting log lay mostly submersed in the dark water, and on the log sat small black frogs. They leaped into the water and disappeared. I was still concerned about my water filter not being sealed correctly, and this stagnant black water was not something I wanted to chance.

"They probably call it Trooper Spring because you have to be a god damn trooper to drink from it and live!" I told myself.

I sat and watched the frogs leap on and off the log for a few minutes, and decided to carry on. My next chance for water would be ten miles away.

After another ten miles I reached "Warm Springs River". Halfmile's notes said it was a "Double log crossing". I stood and stared at the small foot path over the shallow water. The water was maybe a few inches deep, and the bridge was one halved log and a hand rail to hold on to. It was hardly a river! Three teenage boys sat on the foot bridge, refilling their water. They all looked up at me, but ignored my presence until I said hello.

"How far are you going?" One of them asked.

"Cascade Locks." I answered.

I didn't inquire about where they were going or where they came from. I wanted them to move on, so I could refill my water and make camp.

I left the boys at the log crossing to find a camp site, and messaged Charlie. The wind was blowing, and rain started to fall. The tall trees around the camp area rocked and creaked.

"Made it. sketchy trees. Dark woods. fun stuff. Lol" I told him.

I had gone twenty miles for the day, and was thankful to be done. It was one thing to be hiking so many miles day after day in less than desirable weather, with inadequate water resupplies. But to top it off with the undeniable body aches and fatigue that go along with the inevitable, shape shifting period; I was feeling mostly run over but inexplicably triumphant. And I wanted to curl up in my tent to be alone.

Charlie messaged me back, "How are you feeling?"

It dawned on me, "OMG, I Start my last map tomorrow!" I replied.

I sat and stared at my last section of maps. I couldn't believe it was going to be over soon. I had spent so much time daydreaming and planning for this hike. How could something that took two years to plan be executed in a month's time? It felt like I had just started walking a few days before.

Charlie responded, "Yup you'll be near the base of Hood tomorrow. So proud of you!!!!!"

I still couldn't fathom that I was almost done. But I was excited to be home with Charlie and Cole again, soon.

Day twenty-six

The next morning I got a reasonably early start, and had plans of reaching Mt. Hood by the next day. My power supply was running low and I knew I had to move fast if I was going to keep my GPS tracker up and running. Charlie wanted me to take it easy and urged me to slow down, but I needed to keep things charged. I didn't want my tracking device to go dark, and end up being unjustly sought out by local search and rescue. So, I high tailed it.

Soon Charlie messaged me, "K seriously bb. You are gonna have to slow down or be sitting at Bridge of the Gods for a day or two, waiting!"

I took my time at Timothy Lake and Little Crater Lake. The trail was flat, well kept, and I frequently passed touristy day hikers who carried lattes and other frothy blended espresso drinks; which I would have gladly stolen if it weren't for so many civilized witnesses.

" I am definitely near Portland!" I laughed to myself.

After almost 19 miles I came to my next campsite. I was down to a half liter of water.

I stood on the trail. Thick brush climbed a hill to my left, and to my right was a clearing of campsites. The creek, marked on Halfmile's notes was nearby, but where? I entered the camp area to my right and soon found something etched into the soft dirt in front of me. "Water", it said, with a small arrow pointing south. Beneath it was the number seven with a circle around it.

"Seven has been here!" I said to myself smiling, and followed the direction of the arrow, in hopes of finding water.

"Thank you Seven!" I whispered to myself as I refilled my water bottle from an ice cold trickling pool of water. The location of the small pool would have been difficult to find if it had not been for Seven's arrow that he drew in the dirt. I gathered enough water for dinner and hot chocolate, but I had to get my tent set up before the rain came back.

"Here, use this!" Charlie handed me a rock to pound in the tent stake. I was learning to set up the tent he bought me for Christmas 2012. "Or, you can just use the heel of your boot", he demonstrated, helping me set up my Kelty tarp in the back yard while preparing for my hike. He was full of tips and little tricks to make things easier for me. I was usually full of piss and vinegar and always acted like I could just figure it out on my own. This attitude generally kept me from fully taking in everything he had to say to me.

My Marmot EOS1 sprung to a raised position with little effort. I pushed the first two stakes into the soft ground with ease. The third wouldn't go in by hand, and I gave it a good shove with the heel of my boot. I positioned the fourth stake, and gave it a good tap with the heel of my boot. It didn't go in. So, I stomped on it a little harder. The stake crumbled like taffy. No longer strait, it curved like the letter S and bent to the side; still without going into the ground. I picked up the stake and looked at it mortified.

"Smooth move jack wagon!!" I chuckled to myself.

I was annoyed, but not angry at myself like I was the first few days of making mistakes out here. I repositioned the tent a few inches in another direction, and used the stake the best I could.

Charlie and I messaged back and forth about my plan for the next few days, trying to narrow down when I would get to the Bridge of the Gods. I looked over the notes I had made back at Olallie, and sent him my plan. Thankfully, Charlie was paying closer attention than I was!

"What are you talking about mile 2137?" He asked

"You said your taking Eagle Creek alternate route right? That is 15.4m. Page G-6!"

I looked over my maps again. Shit! I thought, but tried to play it off like I hadn't overshot my alternate route by almost ten miles.

"So Friday I start at 2125 And take Eagle Creek Falls for my final 15 miles?" I wrote.

We agreed on the plan he had sent to me, and I let him know I was exhausted and headed to bed.

"Get some rest bb. You're AMAZING!! I love you." He said, completely ignoring my mistakes. He had a way of encouraging me through my blunders; Something I was beginning to learn to do for myself.

Before long, Road Trip and Trail Dancer came into camp. I watched them for a few minutes, searching with great effort to find the hidden pool of water. I came out of my tent and directed them over to it. They made camp and I returned to my tent to pass out.

Day twenty-seven

I jolted awake around 6AM, and sent Charlie a message "Over slept. 14.5 miles to timberline". Charlie checked the weather forecast for me, and I packed up my gear, except for my toiletries. Nature was calling! I needed to find a secluded area away from my camp neighbors. I crossed the trail, and headed up the hill on the other side. I had left my trowel back near North Fork Mesa in the Three Sisters Wilderness. Ever since, my boot had become my new cat-hole digger.   I found an enclosed area, under some thick trees. The branches had protected the ground from the rain, and the dirt looked soft and dry. For a moment I thought that I may find a different spot, because this looked like prime real-estate for small woodland creatures, or even a nice bedding area for larger ones. However, I was in a bit of hurry.

I placed my tracking device and toiletry bag against the base of a tree, and proceeded to use the heel of my boot to dig a deep enough hole. The dirt was soft, and was easy to dig into. Too easy, I thought.

Before too long my boot hit what felt and sounded like a rotted or hollow log. I stopped digging, and looked around to check for critter holes or any other signs of possible inhabitants. Nothing!

Dropping my britches and hovering over the hole, I set my gaze in the direction of camp and the trail. I had a fear of being stumbled upon while using the bathroom, even out in the middle of the woods.

Crouched, and concentrating on business, I swatted a bee or a fly that had tried landing on my face. At the moment I wasn't sure which it was, and didn't think too much of it! And then another. A second or two later I realized I could hear a faint humming or buzz. Looking down, a few yellow jackets swarmed around my boots.

"What about bees Crystal?" My brother questioned me on the phone, after he went through various scenarios like rattle snakes, rabid foxes, broken bones, and cougars.
"Have you thought about bees?" He continued to scold me.
"I've seen grown men accidentally step through underground yellow jacket nests, and be stung so bad they had to be airlifted out of the fuckin' woods! We Could hardly recognize them after!"
He practically yelled. But he wasn't really yelling. He was using what the rest of the family likes to refer to as "the brother Bill voice". And it took years of Special forces military training to acquire it.
"What are you going to do in that situation?" He demanded!
"I don't know…" I said softly and perplexed, holding back a flood of tears.
"Then you have no business being out there alone!"
My brother Bill was talking me out of a three day solo hike, and for good reason. It was the summer of 2013, and I didn't even know how to properly use a map and compass. I had no tracking device or ability to call for help. And I certainly hadn't entertained the thought of being swarmed by bees! I canceled that trip.

The humming became very loud within seconds, and I looked over my shoulder. Yellow jackets spewed from the ground below me. A black and yellow mass grew into a buzzing cloud around my ankles, and then around my head. I jumped up, tugging on the waist of my rain pants, trying to pull them up while leaping from beneath the tree branches. The bees dove and bounced off my forehead! Running back down the hill I swatted them out of my hair.

"Ouch! Fuck!" I yelled as they stung me, thrashing through the bushes.

I patted down and slapped at my clothes. Before I knew it I was back at my campsite. Trail Dancer and Road Trip stood there staring at me with their mouths open.

"Are you OK?" Trail Dancer asked.

Realizing I was no longer being chased, I took a second to shake out my hair and shirt.

"I just pissed on a yellow jacket nest" I said trying to catch my breath, and I burst into laughter.

I could only imagine how crazy I looked coming out of the woods in a full sprint, and flailing around like I was on fire.

Trail Dancer gave me some bee-sting ointment. The bees had only gotten me three times. Two stings above my hip bones, and one on my belly.

"Crap! I left my tracking device and toiletry bag up there!" I said shaking my head, "I guess I have to wait out the swarm and go back to get it".

After almost forty minutes I had worked up enough nerve to retrieve my tracker and toiletry bag. I started to make my way back up the hill. I stepped lightly, and was careful not to make too much noise. Soon, I spotted my small roll of toilet paper, plastic baggie, and tracker. I could also see about a dozen bees swarming around the hole I had dug above their nest. I slowly stepped forward, fox walking towards my belongings. The fox walk was something else I had learned at survival and tracking school.

I knew the slower I moved the better. I crouched down, walking slowly, toe to heel, and when I got within reaching distance I slowly wrapped my fingers around my toiletries and tracking device. The small swarm became alert, and a few of the bees made a move towards my hand. I snatched up my things and ran back down the hill, jumping over small bushes, and sprinting back to the campsite.

"I got it!" I yelled out to Trail Dancer and Road Trip, who were packing up.

They cheered for me.

I messaged Charlie at 8AM, "Headed out. pissed on yellow jkt nest. Swarmed. Stung a couple times. But totally okay haha just a delay lol!"

After a few miles the trail passed by a large parking area alongside highway 26. There was a large outhouse, and I decided I would stop to use the facilities, since I was interrupted at my first attempt for the day. I took a moment to look at the visitors information bulletin board. There were a few missing persons posters hung up on the board. "Sad"... I thought. Then I realized all of the people had gone missing near or around the area I was now hiking through. It wasn't comforting.

I made my way to the outhouse, but both sides were in use. A truck was parked in front of the small building. Two men stood next to the truck, and soon two more men emerged from the bathrooms. They all looked me over.

"Hey!" I said, making sure to make eye contact with each of them. An attempt to hide my self-induced stranger danger paranoia after reading through all the missing person posters. One of the men nodded at me, and the rest of them piled into the truck. I made my way into the bathroom, and quickly locked the door behind me. After a few minutes I heard the engine start, and the truck drove away.

The parking lot was empty as I found my way back to the spur trail that led back to the PCT. After a quarter mile or so, I heard male voices behind me. I whipped around to face them, and I tried to make myself look as fearless as possible. I was determined to make eye contact! Behind me were two men coming up the trail towards me.

I assessed the two men as they came towards me. It was soon obvious to me that they were section hikers. Their packs were over-sized, stuffed to the seams, and the wore heavy rain gear. Both of their faces were dropped down, watching the trail as they conversed to each other. They were about one hundred feet, or less, away.

"Hello! I shouted out and waved with one arm.

Another attempt at "I see you and I want you to know I know you're there". As if they were wild animals.

The men looked up, and then I realized it was just Chris and James!

"Jesus! We can't get rid of her!" James said sarcastically and the two of them laughed.

"I'm happy to see you too, jerk!" I joked back.

We hiked along together for thirty minutes or so, but it wasn't long before the two of them were far enough in front of me, that I couldn't see them any longer. I most certainly had built up stamina, and was able to hike longer than I ever had before. But faster was not something I had achieved yet. Although I kept pushing and trying.

It was a cold and dreary day. I kept my hands tucked away in the sleeves of my rain jacket, and pulled the cuffs down over my trekking pole grips. The trail was flat. I was becoming increasingly bored, and was soon wishing I could have kept up with Chris and James.

I passed the Twin Lakes trial junctions, and after another mile came to the Barlow Pass trailhead and parking area. I found James and Chris sitting at a picnic table, playing a card game. They invited me over.

Again, I was glad to have the company, and have the opportunity to listen to their hilarious banter and jabs. I drank down a Mountain Dew that I had retrieved from a trail angel stash near highway 26. James Smoked. Chris shuffled cards and looked over his guide book. When it was time to go, we all agreed to follow the trail to the left of the parking area. We had about five miles left to hike before we would reach Mt. Hood and Timberline Lodge.

The trial dropped down and merged with an abandoned dirt road. I opened my Halfmile app and it quickly read "You are not on the PCT."

Chris looked over his guide book maps, and I looked over my printed Halfmile maps. I traced my way back to the parking area on the map. The lines were jumbled close together, and it was hard to tell which way we should have gone or if we were going in the right direction at all!

"All I can tell from the map is that we want to keep right!" I said, "We want to cross highway 35!"

We decided to back track to the parking area, and take a look at our options again.

At the parking area, James found a marked trail that was well kept, and paralleled the Old Barlow Wagon road. After a short discussion and one more look over the maps, we all decided to follow the trail; even though my Halfmile app was still telling us we were "Off the PCT".

I put my phone in airplane mode, hoping to save what little battery I had left. My battery pack was nearly dead, and my charging cord hadn't been working properly since I had left Olallie Lake resort.

After about a quarter mile, I soon realized the trail was taking us farther away from the PCT, and in the wrong direction.

"The highway should have only been a quarter mile from the parking area", I said.

James began his way up the hill, hoping to run into the PCT or the highway. Chris and I pulled out our maps again.

"The highway has to be above us, that way", and he pointed up the hill to his right.

Opening the app on my phone once more, it read "Closest PCT intersection at 51 degrees....." but before I could finish reading it, my phone died. I pulled out my handheld GPS, and hit the power button. Nothing. How could that be? I hadn't used the GPS since Crater Lake!

Frustrated, I pulled out my compass. Chris pulled out his compass too. We both shot a bearing of 51 degrees, and began to climb the steep hill. I scrambled over fallen trees and through thick brush, constantly watching my compass to be sure I didn't get too far off course while making my way over and around the obstacles. I kept Chris in my sights, and soon James was in view just above us. The hill only got steeper, but soon we could hear the sounds of vehicles zooming by in the near distance. We scurried faster towards the sound of the highway. The three of us came to the top and clambered over a railing. Breathless, our feet now on the pavement.

We walked on the road for about a quarter mile before finally seeing the "PCT" sign. We crossed the highway, and made our way back to the trail. I was feeling grateful for the map and navigation training I had received in Search and Rescue.

As we hiked along I imagined myself two years ago, without the training, and how I would have handled the situation if I would have found myself in the same position; if I had taken this trip as planned then. The little bit of knowledge on this day made a big difference in the outcome. Knowing what I know, it is not farfetched for someone to be found just a quarter mile away from safety; dead or alive.

More important to me, I felt like I was able to contribute my knowledge to the solution. Before my training, I would have been a lost female, following two men out of the woods. And I wasn't someone who wanted to rely on a man to get me out of the woods!

Once we were back on the trail, Chris and James trotted ahead of me, leaving me in their trail dust. Timberline wasn't much farther away. The sun had come out, and I was OK with some alone time to soak up my gratitude and the surrounding scenery. The closer I got to Timberline, the more I thought about my adventure soon coming to an end. I didn't want to be done, but I was ready to be home with my family.

I began the steep climb to Timberline, Seventeen-hundred feet up, over the next four miles. Each step was painful. The blisters on my feet had gotten bigger, and I was sure I was going to lose a couple toenails over the next couple days. My back ached. My shoulders burned. And my hips throbbed.

"You know, your birthday is in two weeks!" I thought to myself. "You should totally treat yourself to a nice room and a bubble bath when you get to the lodge!"

I daydreamed..

"A warm soft bed…Room service…Sipping wine while soaking in the tub…"

I was sure that it would be way too expensive…

"How bad could it be?" I argued with myself, "You have totally earned it…Charlie will completely understand…He would want you to treat yourself…Plus, you stink…You smell worse than anyone I have ever smelled!"

And I did stink, I hadn't showered since Sisters, almost eight days prior.

I thought about the showers located in the parking lot of the lodge. I had read about them in the hiking guides. After weighing the pros and cons between parking lot showers and unlimited bubble baths, I made my decision; I will get a room when I get to the lodge. But first I would need to find my resupply package, and a new charging cord. I was able to get my phone back up and running from the power I had left on my battery pack, but the cord seemed to be shorting out.

The trail became softer with each step. I was soon trudging through the all too familiar black and gray sand that signified "volcano nearby", and with each step the trail got steeper. It wasn't long before I rounded the corner and was greeted by the majesty of Mount Hood. She was glorious! I continued on the trail and rounded another corner. In the distance I could see Chris and James making their way to the lodge.

Moving slowly, I finally made my way to a paved pathway, that lead me to the lodges parking area. I had made it to Timberline! Droves of skiers and snowboarders migrated in the parking lot, and tour buses came and went. I walked up the large stone stairway, and entered the lodge through the massive wooden doors. People stared as I passed them by, hardly making eye contact with me. I looked around feverishly for the front desk.

When I found it, my heart sank. Sitting on the small wooden desk was a sign, "No Vacancy."

10. STANK

It was almost 4PM. My planning notes said that my resupply package could be picked up in a separate building, across from the lodge, but they closed at 4:30. I figured I didn't have time to stand in line to inquire about the possibility of a room opening up that evening.   By law, there was no camping allowed on or around the lodge property. I was going to have to make camp, somewhere!

I made my way back out to the parking lot, and into the next building. Other than a few scattered teenagers, decked out in Hurley and DC brand clothing, the place seemed deserted. I followed the stairways and corridors down, and finally found the gift shop. It was 4:10PM. After giving the young shop clerk (who was also decked out in Hurley brand clothing) my five dollars he went to retrieve my package.

While I waited for him to return I searched the gift shop looking for a new charging cord. When he returned with my package I asked him about a new cord.

"Do you carry charging cords?

He looked at me blankly, and then looked at his watch.

"We close at 4:30!" He replied.

Obviously he didn't have the time to answer my question!

"There's another gift shop in the lodge." he said before turning away from me and on to the next customer.

I messaged Chris, "Where are you guys at?"
He text me back and said he and James were in the Blue Ox Bar.
"Can I come be stinky with you guys?" I asked.
"Of course!" Chris replied.
I took the long way to double check the front desk. The No Vacancy sign was still posted.

Finding my way to the Blue Ox Bar was more difficult than finding my way to highway 35. The lodge was a maze of circular corridors and off spurs of museum quality artifact displays. I finally made my way into the small bar; a forty by twenty foot room with a bar and a few tables. Chris and James greeted me warmly, and introduced me to some of Chris' family who had met up with them there. The two men were going to be leaving with the family members, and would be staying at a family cabin for a day or two. It quickly dawned on me, this was really more than likely going to be the last time I would see them on the hike.

Chris and James offered me some of the food they had at the table.
"Here, have some meatballs", Chris tried passing me the hot plate.
"No thank you," I resisted politely, "I'm not that hungry."
"Yes you are!" James insisted.
"I know you're hungry!" He laughed.
But I declined the food until the waitress came over to me.
I ordered a Porter, A small pizza, and a plate of meatballs with marinara. The bartender was kind enough to plug my phone in behind the bar to charge. After finishing the beer, I decided to go back upstairs and check out the other gift shop while I waited for my food to come.

I was finally walking around without my backpack. Even still, guests at the lodge avoided most eye contact with me. Except for the few who smiled and nodded at me. Maybe they knew I was a hiker. My legs were streaked with eight day old dirt, my hair was slicked back into a short greasy, stiff pony-tail and held back with a quarter-buff. I wore basketball shorts, and a Columbia fleece. I felt completely out of place, and was sure I stuck out like a sore thumb. I might as well have been walking around the White House with a bomb strapped to my chest.

I walked into the small gift shop. The shelves were lined with fine souvenir merchandise, Sweaters adorned with Timberline logos, sweet smelling handmade soaps, and crystal trinkets. I stood behind a man in

134

line, and I was praying that the gift shop kept the charging cords behind the counter because I didn't see any on the store shelves.

The man in front of me was slightly taller than myself. He was stocky, and muscular. His short neck was braised red with a sun burn. I stood about two feet behind him. I could smell his cologne; CK One maybe, but more than likely Axe body spray. He chatted with the store clerk and then after a couple of minutes turned and looked at me over his shoulder.

"Can I help you?" He demanded. His DC hat tilted to one side of his boxy head, and the reflective sticker glistened under the pristine brim.

I looked at him blankly.

"Ummm, I'm in line!" I finally choked out, in shock from his abrasive attitude.

"Oh!" He said as though I was troubling him.

He turned to leave the line, getting out of my way and then leaned in close to me. He looked at me in the eye, with a devilish grin, and hollered in front of him to the woman that was with him.

"I don't know about YOU, but someone HERE (He briefly put his face into mine) has some SERIOUS B.O!"

He laughed loudly and looked at the lady, then back to me. The person behind me turned away uncomfortably.

I glanced over at the gift shop clerk and he looked just as stunned as I felt. I brushed passed the rude little man, and approached the counter.

"Do you have charging cords?" I asked, holding back tears.

But I could feel my eyes were beginning to well up, more than I could hold back.

"We probably carry those in the other gift shop, across from the lodge. They are open till 6PM." The clerk stuttered.

I was confused.

"But they told me…" I started to debate.. "Never mind!" and I quickly turned to leave.

I just wanted out of there. Mostly because I was starting to cry.

More people had piled into the gift shop, and I wondered how many of them had heard the verbal attack on me from the Forty something year old jerkwad. I found myself standing in the doorway of the gift shop, scanning the crowd. Was I looking for him?

"Damn right you're looking for him, Crystal!" I answered myself.

"You do not get to let people talk to you like that! You did not walk all of this way without learning to be strong for yourself…And you are going to regret it if you don't say anything to him!"

I was right… And while walking back towards the Blue Ox Bar, I saw his lady friend/wife standing outside of the men's restroom. I stopped about ten feet away, and I waited. The door of the restroom opened and he appeared.

Without much thought or planning out what I would say, I approached him.

"Excuse me!" I said loudly, before he could get any further away. He turned and stared at me blankly.

"Oh, hey!" He replied, with a devious smirk.

"I just want to let you know that I am hiking the PCT…and I walked almost four-hundred miles to earn my STANK (at this point I am almost in his face), and I just wanted to ask you what your sorry excuse was for your stanky attitude?"

The lady he was with raised up a fist bump and said "Oh, right on sister!"

I turned my fiery glare towards her and glanced at her fist.

"Oh, fuck off!" I yelled at her. And I stormed off.

"Well…Crystal…That was saying something," I said to myself, "I don't know if it was the something you needed to say…or if you needed to be rude to the girl…but you certainly said something!" I chuckled to myself, completely in disbelief of what had just happened!

I got back to the Blue Ox, and found my food waiting at the table. I ordered another beer. Chris and James looked me over.

"Are you OK?" James asked concerned.

I was shaking, and moving sporadically. Just then the couple walked into the restaurant and sat at the bar just a few feet in front of our table.

"Ya, I am OK, But THAT guy," and I pointed to the man, "THAT guy just told me I SMELLED BAD!"

The couple turned to look at me, and everyone in the bar turned to look at the couple. I continued telling the story, very loudly, so everyone in the bar could hear. I continued to point my finger, until finally in the middle of it the couple got up and left without a word.

Deep inside my heart and my head I could hear the applauding of my ego and self-worth as I watched them walk out.

"With any hope, he will think twice before being rude to someone again…at least for a while!" I said to myself.

It was time for Chris and James to leave. We hugged goodbye, for most likely the last time, and I stayed in the Blue Ox bar to finish my dinner. Trail Dancer and Road Trip soon walked in, and joined me at the table.

I was still holding back tears, thinking about how rude the man had been to me.

"Are you OK?" Road Trip asked almost immediately.

"Ya," I replied, "It has just been a long day." And I wiped my eyes with my napkin. Trying to hide that I was on the brink of tears again.

It was after 7PM and the three of us decided that it was time to go find a camp area. They had heard from some other hikers that there was an area, hidden by a grove of trees, near the lodge that we could hide out in for the night.

We made our way back up the paved pathway, and behind the grove of trees, where others had already started to make camp. With any luck, the lodge security wouldn't be doing their nightly ATV runs, like we had been warned.

"Do you think they would really kick us out in the middle of the night?" Trail Dancer questioned innocently.

"I am not afraid to cry and make them feel bad!" I laughed.

Day twenty-eight

Morning came just as it always had for the last twenty-eight days. Birds chirping, a gentle breeze flowing through my tent, and my sleeping pad rustling beneath me. But there was one thing different about today, and that was an all you can eat breakfast buffet at the Timberline Lodge!

I packed up my gear as quietly as I could, careful not to disturb my fellow hikers, but with haste. Breakfast would be served at 7AM! I carried all of my gear, plus my full resupply box back down the hill and towards the lodge. My plan was to get things plugged in to charge, have breakfast, take a parking lot shower, buy a new charger, get my resupply of gear put away, and then hit the trail. I was hoping to leave no later than noon.

I found my way up the stairs to the restaurant where the buffet was being served. There were many hikers there. Some sprawled on the couches, hovering over the electrical outlets, some wondering the corridors snapping pictures of the breathtaking architecture, and others bombarding each other with the exciting news of a celebrity at the lodge.

"Hey! Did you hear that Steven Tyler flew in this morning on his helicopter?"

After hearing the news I briefly contemplated that I should skip breakfast and start knocking door to door until I found his room. However, I decided to stick to the original plan, and if he should show up for breakfast I would just bombard him like some crazy stinky homeless fan. And, with any luck he would take pity on me and offer me his shower and room service.

There was another celebrity among us, at least to those of us who were on the PCT, "Billy Goat". Billy Goat is an older man, maybe in his late seventy's, who has spent many years practically living on the trail. Some years he goes north, some years south (this year he was headed south), and other times of the year he may be found hiking long distance trails in other parts of the country. You should Google him, he is pretty amazing! Needless to say, the hikers were all a buzz between Steven and Billy! However, once the waiter came to the large entrance of the dining room and pulled back the velvet rope to clear entry, I lost interest in everything except WAFFLES!

Eggs, bacon, sausage, roasted potatoes, ham, delicate pastries, salmon frittata, and quiche. I piled it all on my plate. I asked the waitress for a coffee and an orange juice. The cream and sugar swirled and blended in the steaming cup of dark coffee. The steam tickled my nose as I held the cup to my lips, and my mouth watered with each sweet sip. I took my time eating, savoring every bite. After almost thirty minutes I turned my attention back to the buffet. The waiter was refilling the handmade whipped cream.

Returning to the buffet, I poured the thick cake-like batter into the waffle iron, and scanned the topping bar. There were apricots, strawberries, blueberries, blackberries, raspberries, peaches, and various syrups. My stomach ached from full plate of rich food that I had just devoured, but I wasn't going to pass up the chance to indulge on this world famous waffle bar. I piled some blackberries and whipped cream on to the fresh waffle, and returned to my table and savored every bite. .

After breakfast, I retreated to the couches that sat around the huge fireplace. I sat heavily, hoping Steven Tyler would appear and offer to rub my belly. After almost an hour of lying there, I decided to head to the other gift shop to buy a new charging cord (which they had, and the new clerk on shift was extremely helpful!), and I soon returned to the couch to continue charging and repacking.

I began to take my belongings out of my resupply box. One by one, sorting them into two piles, "Keep", and "donate to the hiker box". As usual, many of the items except for food, got placed in the donate pile.

"Jesus, Crystal, how many panty liners and batteries did you really think you were going to need out here...you should have packed more Snickers!" I scolded myself.

Then my hand pulled out something I hadn't put in the box before I had left on the trip... A mini bottle of Crown Royal Whiskey. Next, I pulled out a letter. It was from Charlie...

Crystal (2-Sips)

Here it is, your last resupply box. Take a moment to think back to our first resupply...That was hundreds of miles ago! You are almost to the end of this journey. What a great one! You have done something not many can say they have done. You will take with you the memories and stories for the rest of your life.

I have said it many times before but I am so proud of you! Proud of you for not backing down or giving up. For pushing on when you had so many opportunities to say "I'm done". I would have loved to have been with you on this journey, but honestly I don't know if I could have stayed as strong as you. Not to mention, this is your journey, your dream, and your memories to have. We will have our own together.

Inside the box you will find a little gift from me. I didn't suggest the name two sips just to be silly. The night before [I left] I listened to that song (Passenger, Patient Love) over and over. All I could think about was you out there on the trail alone...Saving all the memories and stories till we are back together under the stars. I thought how I was going to miss you.

So, I sent you this [two sips of whiskey] to save until we are together again.

I Love you Crystal. It's your last leg of this trip. Kick ass and savor every moment. See you at the finish line love...

Charlie XOXOXO

It had been quite a while since I had cried on the trail. But, there I was sobbing on a couch in the middle of Timberline Lodge. Trail Dancer checked on me, and I told her about the sweet words in Charlie's letter.

I finished putting away my gear, and stepped outside for some fresh air; with hopes the cold wind coming off the glacier would calm my puffy eyes. It was almost noon.

A couple approached me while I sat in the sunshine on a stone wall, admiring the magnitude of Mt. Hood.
"Excuse me," the man said, "I don't mean to interrupt your peace and quiet. But are you hiking the PCT?"
Instantly I was reminded that I still needed to shower!
"Ya...well...the Oregon section." I answered him.
He and his wife were wanting to hike the Appalachian trail next summer, and they had a few questions about gear and food planning. Before leaving me the woman turned and questioned me,
"So, what has been your biggest take away?"
I smiled, and I thought back to Charlie and I caught up in the storm, me hiding under a picnic table, the lava fields, my mom's support, the amazing green shooting stars, pissing on yellow jackets, Charlie's thoughtful words of love and encouragement, and all of the wonderful friends I was making.
"It's hard to sum up," I started to answer, "but, If I had to,"
I held back the words as I started to choke on the lump in my throat.
"That everything is going to be alright," I continued,
"I mean, nothing on this trip has worked out as planned, AT ALL.. But, It has worked out," I stared at my reflection in the women's sunglasses.
"I suppose life is like that, and I just haven't been seeing it that way. But, it makes more sense to me now." I nodded, confident in my answer.
The couple thanked me for my time and walked away.
I remained sitting on the stone wall and assured myself, "Ya, it is all going to be OK."

I could hardly believe it was almost one in the afternoon. My battery pack wasn't quite charged all the way, but everything had enough power for the final three days of the hike. It was time to go.
I gathered up my gear and said my goodbyes to Trail Dancer and Road Trip. I shook Billy Goats hand, and gave a blanket farewell to the rest of the group.
After leaving the lodge, I made my way back to the trail, past the ski lifts, over a small glacier fed creek, and commenced to climbing steeply up a sandy scree trail.

11. SPIRIT

Breathless, I stopped at the top of the climb, and put my weight on my trekking poles with my head down. The peak of Mount Hood appeared over my right shoulder. I panted, watching the sweat drip from my forehead and on to the ash and sand that made up the trail that carried me away from Timberline Lodge.

"Hey there!" A man's voice called out.

I looked up to see a large group of tourists decorated with plaid, Khakis, over-sized sun hats, and brand new day packs.

"Will you take a group photo for us?" he hollered to me.

I gulped down my breaths, practically gasping. I couldn't hide the "what the fuck?" look on my face.

"Sorry, Probably wasn't expecting that!" he snickered.

I gave him a big smile and said "Of course! Can you take mine too?

"That is quite a pack!" One of them said.

"How long will you be out here?" Another asked.

I filled the group in on where I started, how long I had been out, and where I would finish. Again I was given the usual response by a woman in the group, "Wow, I could never do that!

"You'd be surprised," I smiled, "You've just never tried."

She smiled back at me, but also unable to hide her own "what the fuck?" look.

"Would you like a couple of bananas?" She offered. "They are turning brown and will probably get thrown away!".

I gladly accepted the fresh fruit gift, and realized immediately how yellow and perfect it was.

I continued on to the Zig Zag river, and sat down on the rocky shore. I laid my gear on the banks near the rushing water, and I took my boots off to inspect my blisters; they were burning.

A group of young men crossed the river and blazed up the trail. Before too long I caught up with them while they were taking pictures of the view. I introduced myself, mostly because they were hiking with a pit-bull, and they invited me to hike along with them for a while.

Soon the trail suddenly ended at a sandy cliff that overlooked one of the deepest canyons I had ever seen. We all stood there in amazement, taking in the waterfalls cascading far below us. The water brown and murky, like coffee and cream crashing onto the rocky bottom of the canyon, hundreds of feet below us. I looked around us, desperate to track down the spot we had lost the trail. The trail seemed to have disappeared. I looked down. I was standing on a fragile looking lip at the edge of the cliff, and to the left seemed to be the only way to go on. I quickly suggested to the group that we should space ourselves out, so we don't put too much weight on the lip. The last thing I needed was for someone to have to make that phone call to my family; or theirs.

We followed the edge of the cliff for a hundred feet or so, sometimes with only enough room to put one foot in front of the other. I held on to the small shrubs that lined the sandy lip. We dipped down into over grown blueberry bushes and pine saplings. It wasn't long before I could hardly see the person behind me, or in front of me. I turned on my Halfmile app and sure enough, NOT ON TRAIL. Our choices were to go back to the cliff or keep bush-whacking in hopes to find the trail again.

Crashing down through the bushes, things finally started to clear out, and we finally found ourselves on the trail again.

"You know the last time I got lost, I was with a group of men too!" I joked at the guys.

It was almost six miles to Sandy River. A river crossing I had been dreading since I had first read about it a year or more before. It was another glacier fed river, and I knew the earlier I tried to cross the better my chances of not getting wet (or swept away) would be. The guys and I flip flopped along the trail, and ended up at the river about the same time. They made their camp, and I went to the river to decide if I would keep going.

It was now almost six o'clock in the evening. I messaged Charlie, "Not too sketchy, but I think I will camp and cross in the morning".
I found a secluded spot on the river bank to set up camp, far enough away from the group of men so I could feel alone. I was feeling a little overwhelmed by all the peopley-people at the lodge.
I ate my left over Blue Ox Bar Pizza for dinner, and looked over my map until the sun began to set. Before climbing into my tent I messaged Charlie, "Gonna power down and get ready for bed bb. Missing u ". Laying down in my tent I read Charlie's letter over and over again until it was too dark to see. I made sure my phone was plugged into my battery pack, and tucked it away in my dry sack. A raven cawed out from a tree branch high above me.
"Good night Raven." I whispered... and I closed my teary eyes to sleep.

Day twenty-nine

I was up and packing by 6AM. The Raven perched in a tall tree above my camp site. He cawed occasionally.
"Good morning Raven!" I said and waved a hello into the tree above me.

The Sandy river raced nearby, but it sounded more gentle than it had the evening before. Even though the sky was blue, I put on my rain gear over my clothes. I put everything in my pack except for my knife, para-cord, and tracker. If somehow I went down and my pack got swept away during the crossing, I would have what I needed to be OK until help arrived.

I gathered my battery pack, still attached to the charging cord and pressed the power button to check its battery life. It didn't light up! I pressed it again, and I quickly realized that my OLD charging cord could stay plugged in to the battery pack and phone, and automatically quit pulling power from the battery when the device was fully charged... But my NEW cord had drained my battery pack overnight... I gasped... I took a deep breath trying to calm myself.

"If you have learned anything it is you will either figure it out or it will work out..."
I messaged Charlie at 6:40, "Headed out, will be crossing soon."

143

I looked up into the tall dead tree that the Raven perched in…
"Alright, ready to do this!" I whispered to the bird, "Thank you!"

I always thanked the animals when I saw them. I felt it necessary
to offer my gratitude to them, even if all they did was show up. There
aren't a lot of people who are able to really show up in our lives. It is
important to be grateful to those who do. And this bird, well, it was
there when I went to sleep and was there when I woke up; it had an
entire world it could have been flying around. Instead it stood watch
over me all night. It felt right to acknowledge the fact.

I had read that the farther up the river you went, the easier the
crossing would be; especially early in the morning. I began my way up
stream. Soon I heard the familiar caw above me. I stopped and looked
up, "Hello friend", I said to the Raven. He cawed and swirled high
above me, then landed on the rocks about thirty feet in front of me. I
took a few steps and he took flight. I watched him circle, and then land
again a few yards away from the first spot.
"Do you want me to follow you?" I asked the Raven, as if it knew
what I was about to attempt the river crossing.

I approached the river and scanned the area for a safe place to
cross. Nothing here. Then, the Raven cawed again, circling and
landing on a giant boulder fifty or more feet away. It cawed and
flapped its wings. Something in my gut told me to listen.

I made my way towards the Raven, who now sat silently on the
boulder, patiently watching me get closer. Only thirty feet or so
separated us, I looked to my left at the river.

Low and behold, a pile of small logs had become dammed up on
the river bed. The logs stretched all the way across the river! I could
tell that once the water rose by afternoon, they would be submerged
again, hidden away. I looked to the Raven, who still sat on the boulder
watching me.
"Thank you!" I said. Gratitude swelled in my chest.

In perfect timing the Raven flew away, towards the spot I had
made camp the night before. I watched him until he was out of sight.

I focused my attention on the crossing. The logs looked sturdy
enough, but just in case I used my trekking poles to test the integrity of
the logs before each step. Once I made it across I peered out into the
trees, searching for the Raven.
"How fricking COOL was THAT!?" I said out loud.
"That was amazing, NO ONE is going to be able to understand what
just happened here!"

But I knew! And I thought it was magical! I messaged Charlie, "Didn't have to get in, followed a raven logs about a quarter mile up stream! "

"Nice! Work smarter, not harder", he replied.

I arrived at Ramona falls about thirty minutes later. I stood there in disbelief, looking at my surroundings and the water gushing from the rock in front of me.

"Seriously! Are you serious right now? This is your life... You're seeing this right now...LOOK at this!" I was beaming!

I sat and had breakfast (that is code for trail mix and a Snickers bar) in the dirt in front of the falls. I snapped some pictures and started down the well-kept Ramona Falls Trail (alternate from the PCT).

Giant tree roots gushed and plunged from the forest floor. A clear fresh water creek flowed deeply along the trail. It looked to be two or three foot deep. Millions of small pepples lined the bottom of the creek, and it rippled gently.

Soon, spongy moss blanketed the earth around me like a lime green pillow top. I was sure, in that moment, that if I could describe heaven it would be like this place. But after only two miles, I emerged and found myself back on the Pacific Crest Trail.

Without much time to think or worry about it, I found myself at the Muddy Fork double log crossing. It looked simple enough, until I began to cross it. There was one large log to step on, and then a second log over the top of the first log to hold onto. A climbing rope was tethered to the top log to hold on to for safety. I stepped on to the bottom log, and soon realized that my pack took up too much room, and I had to turn my body to the side, inching and slinking my way across. The river rushed rapidly about ten feet below me. I made my way across, and climbed up and over the root ball that was the end of the makeshift foot bridge.

I stopped to take a look at my map, and saw that I was about to begin my last "big climb" for the entire trip. On the topo map it looked like I was about to make my way up a rather steep but steady mountain side, and then through a series of switch backs (cut into a cliff) towards Bald Mountain.

After about seven-hundred feet up, I could hear voices ahead of me. I stopped for a moment, listening to the sounds of chatter. I continued on. Finally around a switch back I came across three hikers.

Two men, and one woman. They had stopped at an on-trail stream to refill water.

"Hello!" I said, and continued on.

It wasn't long before I noticed one of the men gaining on me.

"If I slow you down," I hollered behind me, "let me know and you can pass, (big deep breath) these hills slow me down".

He assured me it was fine, but I stopped at the rounding of the next switch back to let him and the other male hiker pass me by. Soon the female hiker wasn't far behind me. I stopped to turn and look at her, to see how far behind me she was. I didn't want to hold her up as well. She marched, her gaze held steady on the trail in front of her. Left...Right...Left...Repeat... I knew that cadence all too well. She was strong, I could tell, especially mentally. Her mind focused on the prize.

I had seen a lot of women out here on the trail, but most of them thru-hikers, or section hikers that had a lot more experience than myself. Those hikers had the advantage of hundreds and hundreds of miles beneath their feet, and it gave them the endurance to practically run through Oregon. There was only one other woman I had seen out here with the magnitude of perseverance draped on her brow like this woman, and that was me...And I instantly felt connected to the women coming up the trail; like a kindred-spirit. She marched behind me. Our packs rocked and clanged. Our boots stirred up dust, and the aroma of sweet pine and forest floor filled the trail space between us.

At the next switch back her male counterparts waited. She and I arrived together, and I introduced myself. They also introduced themselves. Their names: Snake Jumper, Magic Man, and... Shaun.

I joked with Shaun that maybe I could name him by the end of the day.. "Maybe," I said, "your name could be 'by the end of the day". I laughed.

The group of three were from Nevada, and the trip was for Snake Jumper's birthday. I thought it was an amazing birthday trip, a PCT section hike. We chatted for a bit, and then hiked on. We flip flopped for a bit and then I stopped for lunch. I sat and ate a pouch of tuna fish, and swatted away the biting flies.

"I'd rather deal with mosquitoes", I thought out loud, "I have spray for those!"

The three hikers passed me by, while I rested.

After another couple of miles the terrain turned from thick forest to flat and covered in stubby manzanita and madrone. The trail was dry, and the sun was hot. I could hear chatter in the distance, again, and found the three Nevada hikers tucked away at a picnic table in the shade. They invited me to sit. Snake Jumper gave me some of her dehydrated watermelon (homemade). It was absolutely, hands down, the best thing I had eaten in the last few weeks, second only to the waffles at Timberline!

At one point I raised my arm above my head to fix my head band or something, and realized I had just shown off my arm pit hair (which was now almost an inch long)… But, it turns out, none of them either cared or noticed, and the three of us hiked along towards Lolo pass.

We followed a dirt road, parading close to the shoulder to avoid the large construction trucks that occasionally passed, and we finally found the trailhead after a long period of uncertainty.

We stopped to refill water at another switchback. The water trickled down the side of the hill, and pooled in rocky patch next to the trail. After our containers were full I picked up my pack and placed it on my knee, preparing to heave it over my shoulder and then onto my back.

Magic Man turned to me, "Do you need help with that?" he offered.

Then he chuckled, "Nah, you probably got it OK if you've been doing it yourself after all this time!"

I smiled and nodded at him to confirm, "Thank you though!" I said. Finally, a man that understood I wasn't helpless just because I was a female!

Their plan was to go to as far as Lost Lake for the night. They had heard or read that they would find pizza and beer there. As tempting as it sounded, my plan was to go a little further, to "Salvation Spring", before camping for the night. It wasn't that much further up the trail from where they were headed.

When I finally arrived, I found two male hikers sitting near the spring, and they greeted me with waves and nods as I made my way from the brush encroached trail and to the clearing. The trail itself came to a head at the small trickling stream. I stood there to take a look at the water. It would be enough to drink from, it looked clean enough, but it was only a few inches deep in most parts, and only about a foot across for most of its visible length. Thick grasses and blueberry bushes took over the banks.

I put my pack down against a large punky log, and retrieved my water bottle and filter from the side pouch. The two men sat on the banks, still chatting. I walked over to them and sat down with them as if I had known them all of my life. They looked at me awkwardly, but then continued their discussion about pack weight, miles per day, and water consumption.

They never really spoke to me, other than when they got up to leave. "Have a good hike!" One of them said. And they left.

I sat there on the muddy bank and dug down into the stream bed to make room for my water bottle. The biting flies buzzed around me in thick swarms. I tried to ignore them, but the longer I sat there, the more they tried to feed on me. With enough water to cook with for the evening, I went back to where I left my pack to find a suitable camp spot.

Nearby, behind the log, was a large clearing to set up my tent. It was early, much earlier than I had ever stopped for the day, but I had to stop in order to stay on the schedule Charlie and I had agreed on. Tomorrow would be my last night out here. Since Timberline, this was the first night without anyone around. The first time without so much as a distant human voice, or presence. The quiet fell heavy on me.

I messaged Charlie at 4:30PM, "Lonely stopping so early in day. Camp is set though".

He replied, "Lonely here waiting for you too."

My heart sank.

12. SALVATION

I wanted to keep going for the day, I was feeling restless. I wasn't sure if I was feeling so down because the trip was almost over or if I was home sick. I was ready to be home with my family, but I was far from ready for my hike to be done. And Salvation Spring was proving to be far from a deliverance. Between my heavy heart and the thick swarms of biting flies it felt more like melancholy. I curled up in my tent, and zipped it up to keep the flies out. But the longer I laid there the sadder I got.

I started thinking about the Army survival book my brother had lent me, **"Loneliness and boredom can be a source for depression. If you are alone, you must find ways to keep your mind productively occupied... You must have faith in your capability to go it alone".** It was clear to me that I shouldn't just sit there feeling miserable waiting for the sun to set.

I got up and took my toiletry bag to the creek. I washed my face, legs, and underarms. I then washed my socks and underwear. I found a large tree branch and hung my laundry from its dead limbs, and propped it against a large tree in the sun. I made dinner, and a cup of hot coco. I watched and listened to other hikers traveling by above me on the PCT. They were at least reassurance that I wasn't really alone. When the sun began to move, I moved my laundry with it. I read my maps and map notes. I picked blueberries and watched the squirrels scamper and forage through the thick blueberry bushes that surrounded my camp.

Before I knew it, it was 7:30PM.

Charlie messaged me, "FYI bb your camped out on the 400 mile point!!! Xoxo".

I laid back down in my tent, watching the swarms of flies grow thicker as the sun light disappeared, and I tried to fathom what four hundred miles really looked like. What it felt like. But I drifted off to sleep before I could completely absorb it.

Day thirty

I jolted awake around 5:30AM. I sat up and looked around my tent for my tracker, I hadn't messaged Charlie back the evening before. I hadn't even brought in all of my laundry before falling asleep. I peered out of my tent to check that the squirrels hadn't carried off my socks and underwear. I unzipped the tent and clambered out slowly. Everything was where I had left it.

The rising sun danced in the trees around me. The towering dark green conifers glowed with remarkable hues of red and gold.

"So, this is what a four-hundred mile sunrise looks like", I smiled and took a deep breath while closing my eyes, "Thank you", I whispered.

I gathered my gear, and was getting ready to go when I heard someone coming down the Salvation Spring trail. I stood there watching, waiting for them to appear through the brush. A man emerged. He wore a pale blue exofficio type shirt, light tan khakis, and a ball cap. He was older, tall and thin, and when he took off his cap he exposed his white freshly trimmed hair. He was far too clean to be a thru-hiker, I thought, but his pack was an ultra-light pack, and it looked like it had seen more miles than most packs. But he was still too far away for me to really tell.

"Good morning!" I called out to him as I flung my pack onto my back.

He turned towards me and took a long stare.

"Oh, hello! thought I'd be alone down here!" he hollered back.

My heart leaped, I knew that voice!

"Seven?" I squeaked back, my voice cracking.

"Yep!" He answered, sounding slightly confused.

I tried not to run to him.

It had been rumor that Seven had gotten off the trail, and I hadn't seen any sign of him since before Crater Lake until I saw the number seven etched into the dirt just after trooper spring. All but rushing to him I tried to explain who I was as I approached him.

"It's me, Crystal, well now its Two-Sips, my husband Charlie and I met you at Christie Spring, he's not with us anymore...I mean, he's OK, he had to go back to work after Crater Lake... Oh my gosh, I thought you had gotten off trail because of your hip.." I reached him, still adjusting my chest strap and hydration line.

Seven stood grinning at me.

I soon realized I was rambling, and I gave pause so he could compute what I said through my excitement, and respond.

"Yes," he finally answered, "I do remember meeting you and your husband! Do you want to hike along with me today? I'd like the company".

Inside I exploded! So many of the hikers I had met spoke about Seven, and everyone had a theory to Seven's elusive past. Was he a CIA agent? Was his hip injury really an "old sports injury", or did he get injured on a secret mission? Why didn't he let anyone take his picture? Why didn't he tell anyone where he was from? Did he really summit the world's seven highest peaks, and that's how he got his name...? Maybe Seven is short for Double-0-7, and not The Seven Summits..?

"Yes! I would love to hike with you!" I replied almost instantly, "Just don't let me slow you down!"

Seven smiled at me, "This old sports injury I have been rehabbing keeps me at a slow and steady pace, I doubt you'll hold me back", he said softly.

We hiked out together, but Seven had me go ahead of him. The trail climbed gently but steadily. With Seven behind me I moved a little faster. He had come all the way from the Mexican border. Injured or not, he was sure to be a faster hiker than I, and I didn't want to get in the way and have him decide to leave me behind!

He did most of the talking as we walked. He told me about the friends he was making along the way, the stops he made. The time he did get off trail to spend some time in Portland; seeing a doctor for his hip. He talked about sports, a lot about sports! I tried to keep up.

"Do you like Basketball?" He inquired.

"Mmmm? I used to," I answered, "I mean, in high school my boyfriend and his friends were really into it. I used to keep up with a few of the teams. I knew all their names, jersey numbers, rankings... I guess I figured if I was going to be hanging out with them I should probably be able to be a part of the conversation.. you know, be a good girlfriend. But that was almost twenty years ago!"

Seven kept talking, and used basketball as a segue to tell me about the New Golden One arena being built for the Sacramento Kings.

Soon we stopped on the trail to take in the surrounding view. In the far distance I could see Mt. St. Helens, Mt. Adams, and possibly Mt. Rainer. I stood in deep thought for a moment standing in Oregon and looking out over Washington, and I finally spoke.

"Mt. Saint Helens erupted when my mom was pregnant with me. She used to tell me that when it erupted it was a sign of my coming", I laughed.

Seven chuckled and then asked, "What did you mean when you said you watched basketball to be a good girlfriend".

Taken back by the question I answered, "I think what I really meant was being an attentive girlfriend... I didn't just want to be a girl on his shoulder. When my husband and I were dating, I got into dirt bikes because he liked to ride them... Well, I dabbled in crashing them, actually. I figured if I learned too, then we could spend more time together doing what he liked to do..."

Seven took some jerky from his pocket, never taking his eyes off me. "Did you ever figure out what you liked to do"? He asked with burning intensity in his eyes.

"Ya", I started to get a little choked up, "I like to hike", I said.

Seven smiled while chewing, "And here you are!" He said after a short pause. And He held his hands out to his side, as if I had arrived.

"And here I am!" I said quietly looking back at the view.

And we kept moving.

We had covered almost eleven miles in a little under three and a half hours. We arrived at Indian Spring campground right at 11AM. This was the campground I was supposed to stop at for the day, and then continue on to the Bridge of the Gods the next morning. I hadn't expected getting there so soon in the day.

The parking area was barren. The Halfmile notes said there was an abandoned piped spring nearby. But where? Seven and I looked over our maps and water notes, then agreed to split up, searching the spur trails in the old campground. We found nothing but an abandoned outhouse, and some overgrown dried creek beds.

"Well, there will be plenty of water on the Eagle Creek trial," Seven said, "I don't think you should stay here alone tonight. I'm worried it will get you depressed. And you do need water."

I thought about how lonely I had been the day before, and I was now very low on water. But I hadn't mentioned the spell of loneliness I had experienced the night before, to Seven.

I messaged Charlie, "No water here . Have to move on".

Seven and I began our decent to the Eagle Creek trail. After about a quarter mile we came across the abandoned piped Spring. A small rusted metal pipe protruded from a block of concrete in the side of the hill.

"I am glad I decided to keep going with you!" I told Seven.

We refilled our water and continued on.

"You wouldn't have liked that old campground anyway", He said.

I had water now, I could have turned around to make camp. But I wasn't ready to stop for the day. Plus, there was something about Seven that made me feel calm and grounded. He felt like a father figure to me.

"Oh! My father", I shouted back to Seven, reminded by the comparison. Seven turned to listen to me.

"I have my dad's ashes with me... I wonder, if I find a spot on the EC trail, would you take some pictures for me while I spread them?" I asked him.

"Sure, I would be honored to do that for you," he agreed.

The trail plunged, we descended almost two thousand feet in under two miles. The tips of my toes and my shins were on fire, but I pushed on with Seven now close behind me.

The trail finally leveled out and the scenery suddenly turned into a different world. Thick spongy moss and ferns covered the ground, stubby trees with large star shaped leaves; their branches intertwined with thick vines and moss. Small waterfalls appeared every thirty to one-hundred feet, and I could hear the rushing Eagle Creek below us. The air was thick and humid, and I was suddenly sweating profusely. Seven and I stopped periodically to splash water on our faces, and gulp down ice cold water from the pools.

He continued talking as we walked along. He told me about his sister, who lives in another state and works for a university. He told me which city he lived in, he told me what he used to do for a living before he retired, and he told me about how he doesn't have a cell phone, for "nontraditional" reasons. Nor does he use the internet,

153

except to check his email once a week because, "it's just the way the world works now".

We talked about me wanting to get better at running, and he coached me on how many times a day I should train, and how my routine will be dramatically different from preparing for long distance hiking. He was full of knowledge, no matter the topic. And he made me feel like I had known him for years and years. During the quiet moments, which were few and far between, I thought about the purpose of our meeting. I contemplated the lesson I was supposed to learn from Seven. Was it a coincidence that I met back up with him at a spring named Salvation?

Soon, the trail turned into a jagged rock path that ran along the side of a sheer cliff. I had read about it, and feared it from the beginning. I was deathly afraid of heights, but somehow being there and coming all this way, I walked confidently; peering out over the cliffs to see the magnificent Eagle Creek below me.

Suddenly, rounding a corner, I stopped frozen with amazement at what I saw. Tunnel Falls cascaded over the mossy cliffs. One-hundred sixty feet tall, its water crashed and swirled into a large pool below. I turned to Seven.

"This is it!" My eyes swelled with tears, and it took everything I had not to begin sobbing.

I set my pack down, shaking, I dug down deep into the main compartment and pulled out my father's ashes.

"I think this is really a remarkable spot, he would be really pleased," Seven said as I prepared.

I sent a quick message from my tracking device to my family, "Leaving Dad here."

My mom soon messaged back, "Say a prayer for me".

I handed Seven my phone, and showed him how to take a picture. He fired off some practice shots, and said "I think I got it."

I walked slowly towards the waterfall, and stood as close as I could to the tunnel that disappeared behind it.

The waterfall created a wind that swirled up from the pool below me, rays of sunlight danced in the mist and spray, and rainbows levitated all around the canyon. I closed my eyes and I pictured my father's face.

"I pray you are in peace where ever you are dad… Thank you for coming all this way with me…Thank you for going as far as you could with us while you were here…Thank you from all of us…See you again…"

I used my knife to cut open the thick plastic, and began to pour the ashes over the cliff and into the swirling mist. Tears ran down my face until the bag was empty. I stood and watched the ash mix with the mist and rainbows until I suddenly felt a hand on my shoulder.

"I think I got some good pictures for you." Seven said softly.

"Thank you", I said while wiping down my face.

"Can I get your picture next to the falls for you? I asked him. I can email it to you."

Seven's eyes widened, "Oh no, I'm camera shy!" He smiled nervously and he stepped to the side.

I took a couple more pictures of the waterfall, and Seven stood back away from view. We continued on for a couple more miles before finding an available camp site.

There was a couple already in the large camp area, and I recognized them from the group at Timberline. I noticed that they had a battery charger, and they let me plug in my dead battery pack. I didn't need much, just enough to get me through to the next morning. "See? Everything always works out!" I reminded myself.

Seven and I retreated to our tents for the evening. While lying there I thought about how I hadn't showered or shaved in eleven days, and how awful I was going to look when Charlie picked me up. I laughed at the thought of what I must look like. What I must smell like. I thought about how nice it had been having Seven's company all day, and what a blessing it was that he was there to document me spreading my dad's ashes.

In the quiet of the evening, Seven called from his tent, "Hey, Two-Sips, you awake?"

"Ya?" I answered and laid there listening.

"Well, I just want to tell you that it was really nice walking with you today… I think your dad is really proud of you…And you picked a good spot for him…Say hello to Charlie for me."

His voice was angelic and calming, I could feel myself drifting off.

"Thank you Seven, I had a nice time too, thank you for everything today…See you in the morning", and I drifted off.

Day thirty-one

Opening my eyes, I looked at the time, 5:15AM. I unzipped my tent and looked to my left, where Seven had put up his tent the evening before. He was gone. There was no trace that he had ever been there. He had told me that he liked to get an early start each morning, but for a moment I questioned if he was even real...

I packed away most of my gear, and went to the creek to clean up. I decided that it was important to me to at least feel cleaner than I was, before seeing my family for the first time in weeks.

I sat on the shore and lathered my handkerchief with biodegradable soap, and ran it across my dirt streaked legs. For a moment I thought maybe I should leave the hair, the dirt, the smell. I should leave it all so when I see my family they can see the trail come out with me.

"No matter how hard you try, you can't wash off what you're about to finish". I said to myself proudly.

I sat on a stump in the campsite, eating breakfast and sipping coffee. I was trying to take my time. I didn't want to be waiting too long to cross the bridge into Washington, and I had promised Charlie I wouldn't cross without them there. Timing was going to be everything!

I thought deeply about the last thirty days, and how it had changed me. I was afraid for the journey to be over. I wasn't sure if I was really ready. "But you are ready... You have always been ready... You just didn't know it"... I told myself. Maybe I did always have what it took, or maybe something new inside was ignited and I found it out here. The truth of the matter is that I had felt something inside of me die miles and miles ago...days and days ago. I felt a little bit of it go every time I surrendered to the suffer. And every time a part of me would wither away, something more spectacular would begin to grow to replace it. Just like the purple lupine that sprung to life in every one of the burnouts I trudged through.

While I sat and pondered, I dictated a mental letter to Charlie:

Dear Charlie,
I am writing to let you know that I won't be coming back! I am not sure what it was that drew me to the trail...Or what it was that made

*me want to hike so far. I am not sure what kept me going out here
for so long, but you need to know that I am far too weak to leave
now.*

*I am sending someone to you, to replace me. You will find her to be
stronger, more clever, and more determined than I ever was. She will
love you more than I can, because she knows what it is like to fully
appreciate you . She will be a better mother, because she knows what
it takes to grow . She is inspiring, and she is braver than I ever
imagined myself.*

*When I was clutched to self-doubt and wanted to quit, she showed
up to carry me farther. I believe it is fair to say that she is the one
that deserves to finish this journey.*

*I am sorry that I cannot come home. But she has promised to take
good care of all that is ours.*

Sincerely,

Crystal

P.S They call her Two-Sips

I finished putting my gear away, and flung my pack onto my back.
I messaged my family, it was 8:30, "Final 8 miles".

The Eagle Creek Trail is a path that cuts into jagged rock. You
cross a series of foot bridges, pass multiple waterfalls, and pools of
cool water. It is a popular day hiking area, and I often stepped to the
side so that others could pass.

One group of women stopped me on the trail, "That is quite the
backpack", one woman said to me.

"I get that a lot!" I chuckled.

I began to tell them how I was hiking the Oregon section of the PCT..
And so on and so forth.

"Oh wow! So you're doing the same thing as that one Wild lady,
right?" She asked with amazement.

I bit the side of my cheek, "No.. No it isn't really like that at all.." I
began to answer her, especially irritated by the continued comparison
to Wild.

Not because I don't love the story, I do, but because I was living my
own story, not someone else's. And I wanted it to be more clear to
people.

"I mean maybe kind of.." I retracted, "but I didn't hike as many miles... and actually my story involves a lot less sex and heroin"... I answered sarcastically.

The woman's mouth gaped open, and I grinned.

"Well, be safe!" she said to me and the three of them hiked away, whispering and looking back at me.

Soon I passed another woman who was with a man, and she stopped me, "Excuse me... how far is it to punchbowl falls?" She asked.

"Less than a mile", I said to her.

"Are you hiking the PCT?" She inquired.

"Yes..." I said cautiously (Jesus, please don't ask if I am like that Wild lady!).

"Are there any other hikers behind you?" She asked.

"No others that I have seen this morning." I answered. And I wondered again if Seven had been a figment of my lonely imagination or a guardian angel of sorts.

The woman turned to walk away after thanking me. I turned back and hollered to her, "Wait, What are their names?"

She thought for a moment and said "Probably going by Snake Jumper and Magic Man".

I instantly lit up.

"I haven't seen them this morning, but I did meet them a couple days ago. I am sure they aren't too far behind me!"

It felt strange, making the transition from the trail and back to real life. It was even stranger to me the way it felt for other hiker's real lives to be colliding with mine. It felt like a completely different universe out on the trail, but now everything was starting to swirl together.

I arrived at the Eagle Creek parking area, and sat down on a bench to eat a handful of almonds. A small group of day hikers gathered around the information board near me.

"The Lord speaks to us in different ways", I overheard one of them say.

An alert from my tracker startled me.

Charlie messaged me for an update, "How ya doin bb?"..

"Great", I responded, "At EC parking lot. Having second breakfast and tourist watching".

However, I wasn't sitting because I wanted to people watch. I was really just trying to kill time.

Charlie messaged me back, "Holy shit!!! Slow down! You're already at the gorge."

He was just passing Eugene, and let me know he would be a little less than three hours.

After some indecisive navigation through the parking lot and help from local tourists, I passed a hatchery and made a right, following a paved path along highway 84; keeping my eye out for Charlie to pass me on the highway. The historic trail (actually it is mostly a historic highway) led me passed blackberry bushes, up and over some dry thick forest, and finally to the edge of Cascade locks.

I messaged Charlie, "Less than a mile out".

He responded, "Umm ya you're VERY. Close. Go take a nap".

His playful demands only made me more excited to be seeing him.

I let him know I was going into town to grab a soda and charge my battery pack while I waited for him to get closer.

I walked into town, and came across the Cascade Locks Ale house. The waitress greeted me and showed me to a table near an electrical outlet. She gave me a menu, and I almost refused, but then I thought that maybe a bite to eat wouldn't be that bad of an idea, and I still had some time to kill anyway. I ordered a Ruben sandwich with pub fries, an Atlas blackberry cider, and a water.

I had made it through all the fries and half of the sandwich when Charlie messaged me to let me know he was getting closer. I got a to go box, and hightailed it back to the trail.

The trail dipped down in front of me towards the toll area for the bridge. I stood there for a moment, staring at the exact place where the dirt-trail met the paved road about sixty or so feet in front of me. "That's it... right there...that is the end". I turned and looked behind me, gazing through the bushes and trying to fathom the four-hundred thirty miles to the south.

"You just did that!" I thought to myself.

"Time to go home." I whispered with a deep breath.

I took my pack off to dig out my fifty cents for the toll booth.

When I looked towards the cars lining up to cross the bridge, Still zipping up my pack, I saw my mom's SUV pull up. Charlie was driving, my mom was in the passenger seat, and Cole was in the back seat with my sister Renee. I started running down the last sixty feet of the trail, trying to put on my pack.

"Charlieeeeee!" I yelled out, trying to buckle up my waist belt as I ran. I took out my phone from my shirt pocket and messaged him. "Look behind you!" I texted

I stopped so I could see him in the driver's side mirror; he glanced up. I waved my trekking poles, and broke down, half laughing and half sobbing. The line of cars began to move, and so I moved with them, cutting between the cars to get a better view of who all was in the vehicle with my husband. Someone behind me honked, and I turned to see Charlie's dad Joel and Charlie's Stepmother Bev waving and smiling from their own car. I cried harder, smiling from ear to ear. I was so surprised to see everyone!

When I got to the toll booth, the woman in the booth asked if I was hiking the PCT, she then said "Stay to the left and go ahead". She waved me on, not charging me the toll fee.

I walked slowly, one foot after another across the metal grate. Charlie drove ahead of me slowly. Wind gusts hit me and I could feel my pack rocking side to side. I watched the water ripple, one hundred and forty feet below me. I looked up, and to my right I passed a sign, It read, "Welcome to Washington".

Charlie and the rest of my family parked their cars in a turnaround near the end of the bridge. Charlie got out and started to make his way towards me, while everyone waited on the other side. He walked briskly, holding the hand rail as he went, but he walked with determination to get to me.

When he finally reached me, we wrapped our arms around each other. He was shaking and I couldn't help but continue crying.

"I missed you" I managed to choke out.

"I missed you too" he said. He held on to my hand as we made it across the bridge, together.

After a short time of hugging and telling a couple trail stories, my family decided we should get a bite to eat.

"We need to get a cheese burger in you, girl!" My mother in law joked, not knowing that I still had half of Ruben sandwich in my pack.

"There's a pizza place in town that would be good!" I said, still not mentioning the fact that I had just gorged myself at the same restaurant.

Walking into the Cascade Locks Ale house, the waitress sat us down at a large table in the back and we ordered a couple of large pizzas. I flagged down the waitress before she could leave to turn in our order.

"Can I have an Atlas Blackberry Cider and a house salad, too", I asked her.

The waitress did a double take at me. I nodded and winked, knowing she recognized me. Knowing that I just wolfed down a good sized lunch and was preparing for round two.

"You got it!" She smiled back at me.

ABOUT THE AUTHOR

Crystal Hidde, Two-Sips, lives in Southern Oregon with her adoring husband, her loveable teenage son, and her two rescued bluenose Pit-Bulls Kona and Zeus. She is a teacher, and she also volunteers as a member of her local county Search and Rescue. Her regular hobbies include day hiking, backpacking, camping, and daydreaming of her next adventure. She is currently working to build an organization called, "Roots to Ridges", to empower women through backcountry experiences and education.

Crystal and Charlie Day one

Spreading my father's ashes at Tunnel Falls

A Caged Bird

A free bird leaps
on the back of the wind
and floats downstream
till the current ends
and dips his wing
in the orange sun rays
and dares to claim the sky.

But a bird that stalks
down his narrow cage
can seldom see through
his bars of rage
his wings are clipped and
his feet are tied
so he opens his throat to sing.

The caged bird sings
with a fearful trill
of things unknown
but longed for still
and his tune is heard
on the distant hill
for the caged bird
sings of freedom.

MAYA ANGELOU

When I Watched Her Fly Away
Written by Charles Hidde

When Crystal first mentioned the idea of doing the 430 mile trek of the Oregon PCT, alone, I responded like any husband would. Fearful. I was afraid of the unknown, afraid of her being alone, afraid of something happening to her and the feeling of helplessness. As with any good husband it's instinctive to want to be the protector of your wife.

When she invited me to go with her from Ashland to Crater Lake I was excited. Excited not only to share in her journey but also to ease my own insecurities of her being out there alone without my protection.

As we began to prepare meals, gear, and the logistics together, those insecurities started to dissipate. I was amazed at how well Crystal had things planned out already in her head. I Only added little suggestions here and there.

Leading up to our departure she made jokes of "you're not allowed to help me!" And even though it went against every instinct I had, I agreed.

As our trip began we both had lessons to learn as we marched along. The fear I once had inside was turning into enjoyment of being a part of the adventure. I became an observer as Crystal took lead checking the maps, planning our next water supplies, and so on.

Crater Lake began to draw closer and closer, with each mile my mind started to wonder again. After spending the week together, I felt more at peace with everything than the day I first heard of this crazy idea. We were doing it, SHE was doing it. Her years of dreaming about this were actually happening.

Hiking gave me a lot of time to think. Soon I would be leaving the trail, Crystal will be alone, and I would be home. The fear I once had was now replaced with a deep sadness. Sadness that I wasn't going to be with her to share in her adventure, and that I was going to miss her deeply.

The day eventually came. My dad met up with us at the rim of Crater Lake to give me and Slip N Slide a ride back to Medford. We all wondered around the rim a little bit taking pictures, laughing, trying not to think about what was about to come. I could tell Crystal was very emotional also, and I tried my best to hide the deep lump in my throat.

As we made our way down towards the trail I remember two young hikers with the sign hitchhiking to the north end of Crater Lake they were very clean and their packs looked hardly used at all. I wondered to myself Are they hiking the PCT or just hitchhiking? The three of us stood around awkwardly for a couple of minutes and then finally dad got a hug goodbye, Slip N Slide got a hug, and then it was my turn.

We all stood there as we watched Crystal hike up a small incline, go around a bend, and out of sight. She never once looked back, and I know why.

"That's one amazing girl you got there", said my dad, as we slowly turned to head back to the parking area.

My dad, a former backpacker himself of the high Sierras, now an eighty something year old man resembling a mixture of Mr. Magoo and Carl Fredrickson from the Disney movie "UP", patted me on the back. I couldn't really muster up any words just a smile and a nod, with the lump still in my throat.

As the three of us made a slow walk up to the parking lot I stopped suddenly, dead in my tracks. Did I imagine it? I turned to Slip N Slide.

"Did you hear my name being called?" I asked him.

The three of us stood there completely silent. And then we all heard it. "Charlie!" It was Crystal!

I quickly turned and started heading back towards the trail entrance. My mind began to race. Why was she calling out my name? I reached the two younger hikers, who were still sitting alongside the trail.

"Did you hear someone yelling?" I asked them.

"Ya, I think so?" One of them said, confused.

And then I heard her emergency whistle! My heart pounded and so did my feet, back up the trail!

As I was running back my mind began to think of all the worst possible scenarios. The trail was right next to the rim of Crater Lake, did she slip ? Was she inches from sliding down the rim? Was she having second thoughts and wanted to come home with us? All I knew is the three of us were panicked and rushing back to where we left her. As Slip N Slide and myself reached the top of the incline and rounded

169

the bend, Crystal was standing there! You could tell she had been crying from the emotional departure just moments ago but now the look on her face was apologetic, because she could tell by the looks on our faces that we were panicked.

"I forgot to resupply fuel for my stove" She yelled to us.

Slip N Slide and myself let out a huge sigh of relief. Right about that time my dad managed to make his way up the incline and came around the corner. Wide eyed and worried for his daughter in law, he stared ahead fearfully.

"I'm sorry dad, I forgot to get fuel" Crystal told him.

My dad let out a deep exhale of relief and exhaustion.

"We will take care of it," I said

"Look for it in the bear vault on the North side of the Rim Trail. And Just like that she was off again.

We raced up to the lodge looking for fuel canisters, but had no luck. We sat around the parking lot brainstorming ideas of what we could do to get fuel to Crystal before she reached the North end of Crater Lake. Slip N Slide needed to get to an airport, Crystal needed fuel. Both in opposite directions, and our mode of transportation was a 1978 VW camper that never breached fifty-five miles per hour. I made the decision that we all drive back to Medford. I would have to make the trip back to the park to get the fuel and water to her.

Once back in Medford, a fellow search and rescue member offered to host Slip N Slide for the night, until he could fly out the next day. I purchased a new fuel canister from REI, and I loaded up in my truck for the drive back to the North end of Crater Lake to leave the care package in the bear vault that was at the trail head parking.

On the drive back north to Crater Lake I was met with a thunder/rainstorm that was barely navigable. My windshield wipers couldn't even keep pace with the rain falling down. My heart sank thinking that Crystal was out in this alone.

"What have I done?" I thought to myself.

"How could I have just left her in this?"

I had no cell signal, therefore I couldn't bring up her location on her personal locator or send her a message to know if she was all right. "Please god let her be ok!" I prayed.

Shortly after, the clouds parted and blue sky was visible. The rain had stopped, and I had new hope that this storm was no were near her. I reached the North end of Crater Lake. I pulled up to the parking lot where the bear vault was. There was a couple there reading the visitor info signs about the park and the trail. I began loading the jugs of water and the fuel when they noticed me.

"Are you a PCT hiker" they asked.

"No, just leaving a resupply for my wife that is hiking Oregon". I replied proudly.

They were eager to ask questions about the trail and asked to get a photo in front of the sign, for a friend that wanted to hike it. I had only been there a few minutes when I heard someone off in the distance "hey!" The voice called out cheerfully.

And out from the woods walked Crystal! Her rain pants on, rain jacket over her and her pack, and a smile from ear to ear when she realized it was my truck parked there waiting for her.

After trading stories of each other's day, it was time for Crystal to move on. She planned on camping in the campsite only about a half a mile further down the trail. We said our goodbyes for a third time that day and I watched again as she hiked off into the woods. I sat there in my truck for a little while wondering what to do now. I began to make my way back home when only a few miles up the road I ran into the storm that I was previously driving through. Within moments the ground was white with hail. I immediately turned my truck around and headed back to the parking lot where I had parted ways with Crystal.

"What do I do!?" I thought to myself.

"I'm not going to be able to run and check on her every time I am worried about her!"

"Remember, I'm not allowed to help you!" I joked with her on the first day on the trail.

However, I found myself walking down the trail to make sure she was ok. I wasn't breaking any rules, I just wanted to see that she was alright. Maybe she wouldn't even see me!

As I came up over a small hill I could see the green tarp that we had been using for shelter. She had made a small dam of dirt around the tarp on the ground to channel any flooding water. Underneath, I could see Crystal sitting on her bivi sack next to her pack, jetboil stove out, all ready for preparing the evening meal. The storm I previously drove into had missed her by less than a mile. No hail on the ground to be seen. I hesitated for a moment. She hadn't seen me yet. Should I just turn back or should I check on her one last time? I walked a little closer as she began walking around her camp. She looked up and noticed me. Again we both were all smiles. More great big hugs were exchanged.

171

We sat and talked about her camp setup. She had some
ustrations with the tarp. I kind of blame myself, that was the one
thing I did do while we were on the trail together. I was the one who
built our camp set up every night. I admired how she had her camp all
set, despite the difficulties she was having.
"Nice work babe! You got this!" I said, and helped her make some
adjustments to the guy-lines to snug things down.
"Thanks," she replied "wanna stay the night?" she laughed.

Had I not dumped my pack at home I would have taken her up on
the offer to spend one more night next to her and Kiss her goodnight
on the forehead.

The time had come to part once again. For the fourth time today we
hugged. I held on to her tightly.
"If you decide to have me to pick you up tomorrow or three weeks
from now at the end, I'm proud of you no matter what!" I assured her.

We kissed one last time. This time it was me walking off into the
forest. And, for the same reasons earlier that day when she never
looked back, neither did I.

After the Hike and More Acknowledgments!

The car ride home was bitter sweet. I was so happy to be with my family again, and so thankful that so many of them came to show their support at the finish line! But I couldn't shake the sadness that I was no longer on the trail, and I wasn't sure of when I would be returning.

That simple fact made me feel incredibly somber. In addition, driving from Washington to Southern Oregon would take just a few hours; it had taken me thirty-one days to hike it. I tried to explain it to Charlie, "It is just frustrating I am passing it all by so fast now, everything I just did!

I sat in the front passenger seat, starring at the scenery fly past me, and after a couple of hours I began to get restless. Part of me wanted to yell out, "Stop the car!", jump out, and run off into the woods with my pack. But I was headed home, and I had a new mission to plan; get more women on the trail!

My mom talked about how proud she was of me. "I found an old road atlas of your Dad's, and I found the PCT on it... I walked every step of that trail with you!" She said to me proudly. I had felt guilty before leaving on my hike, knowing how uneasy the thought of me being out there alone made my mother. She hated the thought of it. But she found a way she could be with me.

My mother watched over me via my satellite tracker. She could pull up my location on a map, online, and see where I was and how

173

, had been there. She made notes on the atlas, and documented
,a day: how far I went, where I camped, where I stopped for
,nch..etc. It was like she was writing a PCT baby book for me. I will
forever be grateful for the support and love she gifted me throughout
the entire hike.

When I got home Charlie handed me a note, "This was in the box
that the couple at Shelter Cove mailed back for you".

It was from Mike and Brooke. When I had found out that Shelter
Cove did not send out packages, the couple offered to mail my
package of gear home for me. The note read:

2-Sips,

*I hope you made it home safe! I would love to hear how the rest of
your hike went. Mike and I are so impressed that you took on this
challenge! Chat with you soon"*

Brooke

Mike and Brooke, if you are reading this, I want to let you know
just how much that note means to me. And I keep it on the fridge,
where I read it every day! Thank you again for getting my gear home
to me!

Special Thanks

I am so very thankful for all of the people I had in my corner. They
were just as much a part of my hike as the trail itself. My husband, my
mother, my friends, my extended family, and my Search and Rescue
family.

There were nights on the trail I sat alone crying, wanting to quit
and go home. Meanwhile, there was a hoard of onlookers and
supporters on Facebook and through text messages, cheering me on!
Most of this was hidden from my view while I was secluded on the
trail. Once home, I was astounded to log into my Facebook, with an
uninterrupted connection, to see so many people talking about my
hike, and commenting on Charlie's updates. I read every one of them!

Thanks to my mother. For always believing in me, never giving up on me, and watching over me!

My husband. For being my rock and my command center. For dropping everything in a moment's notice to find me a new shelter, and send me weather reports. For the constant uplifting words, and nonstop confidence in me. For embracing my adventurous spirit, and loving me with all that you have.

To my friends and family. Thank you for the encouragement, the well wishes, the love, and the acceptance. For sharing my story, and for believing in me! You really make a girl feel like she could do anything she sets out to do.

To my Search and Rescue family. Thank you for the support and encouragement. Special thanks To Duran, Sue, Eric, and Sargent Richards! Thank you for the weather updates, the dehydrated fruit, and the phone calls made in an attempt to get my gear home, and the incredible plaque I received at my first meeting after returning!

To Tianna. Thank you for opening your home! I appreciate all that you did for me! I loved meeting your family, and spending time with all of you!

To Dr. Thorsen (Chiropractic) and Mandy (LMT). I was in such incredible pain after returning home! After just three visits to the office (In Grants Pass, Ore) I was able to return to normal activity, pain free!

Thank you! Thank you! Thank you!

In the months since I have been home I have been planning new adventures. Perhaps sometime soon I will hike the JMT, or complete the Washington section of the PCT. But the mission I want to complete first is getting more women out on the trail and into the outdoors.

I can't count the times I have been told, "Oh, I could never do that!" And each time I have wanted to reply, "You would be surprised what you can do when you believe in yourself!"

I have been told, "You inspire me!" But the truth is, I am inspired by YOU!